The Athletic Revolution

Jack Scott

THE FREE PRESS
A Division of Macmillan Publishing Co., Inc.
NEW YORK

Collier Macmillan Publishers
LONDON

THE FREE PRESS
A DIVISION OF MACMILLAN PUBLISHING CO., INC.
866 Third Avenue, New York, New York 10022

Collier-Macmillan Canada Ltd.

Library of Congress Catalog Card Number: 71–155098

printing number
3 4 5 6 7 8 9 10

*To the many individuals
whose courage and commitment are helping to make
the athletic revolution.*

*. . . and to Micki, Mike, and Marty
who were there from the beginning.*

"We were born into an unjust
system; we are not prepared to
grow old in it."

BERNADETTE DEVLIN (1969)

Preface

By the late 1960's the revolt in the athletic world had escalated to such an extent that some coaches, only half jokingly, talked about asking for combat pay. Coaches who were hardened to the criticism from fans and alumni that came with a losing season were not prepared to be told by faculty, students, and human rights commissions that they were racist, insensitive, and lacked the ability to communicate. Coaches wondered aloud since when was sensitivity a quality they were suppose to possess. Sensitivity was effeminate: the coach's job was to make men out of boys and to produce winning teams. But the criticism kept mounting, and in the fall of 1969 *Sports Illustrated* came to the defense of coaches with a special three part series entitled "The Desperate Coach."

The student movement, the black liberation movement, and the growing counter-culture all began to have an impact on high school and college athletes during the late 1960's, and this led to an inevitable clash between athletes and their coaches and athletic directors. Since 1967 well over one-hundred athletic programs at major colleges and universities have been rocked by some form of disturbance. Additionally, although athletic departments are facing the worst financial crisis in the history of intercollegiate athletics, many college student governments are beginning to withhold funding they have traditionally given athletic departments. In short, college athletics as we enter the 1970's is facing its most severe crisis.

My two main purposes in writing this book are to shed some light on the reasons for the turmoil in American athletics while at the same time trying to offer an analysis that might assist those individuals and groups who are struggling to bring about constructive change in the athletic world. I have attempted to state the facts fairly but make no claims to impartiality. There will be those who will disagree with my interpretation of the facts, but the facts themselves cannot be denied. Whatever your orientation may be to the continually escalating sports revolt, it is difficult to deny that a revolt is at least simmering. Since 1968 there have been a number of instances throughout the country where coaches have been fired as a result of protests by athletes, and hundreds of instances where athletes have been barred from sports participation by coaches who objected to their personal appearance or behavior. And this is only the beginning.

The most publicized aspect of the athletic movement to date has been the black athlete revolt which included the 1968 Olympic Project for Human Rights led by Harry Edwards. While the Olympic Project for Human Rights failed in its effort to bring about a boycott of the Mexico City Olympic Games, it has had a far reaching effect on American athletics. Among other things, it has served as an impetus for the athletic movement and helped to make clear to the general public the highly political nature of competitive athletics.

My prime concern in this book is with athletic programs in our schools and colleges. Interscholastic and intercollegiate athletic programs are usually a microcosm of the total educational structure within which they operate, and the problems discussed in this book are by no means restricted to athletics. Athletic programs would not be allowed to exist if they did not reflect a value orientation that met with the approval of administrators, alumni, and boards of trustees. Consequently, those individuals struggling to humanize athletic programs should realize that it is unlikely that there will be any real changes in athletics without fundamental change throughout our educational structure on all levels. Simply put, there cannot be *athletics for athletes* without a concomitant emphasis on *education for students*.

JACK SCOTT
Institute for the Study of Sport and Society
Oakland, California
Winter, 1971

Acknowledgments

I, like all authors, am deeply indebted to a number of individuals and organizations without whose assistance and concern this book might never have been written. I could easily fill ten pages thanking everyone I am indebted to, but this is neither practical nor possible. Consequently, though I will limit my acknowledgments to those most directly involved in assisting me with this book, I am also grateful to many individuals and organizations whose names are not included here.

I was either a graduate student or teacher at the University of California at Berkeley while most of this book was written, and I will always be grateful to my teachers and colleagues— Ernest Becker, Herbert Blumer, Paul Heist, John Hurst, and Jack London—for the encouragement and assistance they gave me. The four hundred Berkeley students who were enrolled in a course I taught during the winter of 1970 on the role of athletics in higher education made teaching that course the most difficult yet most rewarding educational experience of my life. In ways I'm sure I have not yet even imagined, I know this book has profited immensely from my involvement with these students.

This book is an outgrowth of a monograph I wrote while working as athletic director for Herbert Kohl's Other Ways School in Berkeley, California, and I'm grateful to Herb for his support and assistance at a time when I needed it. Dave Burgin, executive sports editor of the San Francisco *Examiner,* a man who is unquestionably the finest newspaper sports editor in America, was always willing to assist me the many times I called on him.

Two of the chapters in this book first appeared as articles in

Ramparts magazine, and *Ramparts* has thoughtfully given me permission to reprint them here. I have served as *Ramparts* sports editor for the past few years, and I wish to thank the magazine's staff, especially my editor Peter Collier, for giving me the opportunity to travel throughout the United States and to the Mexico City Olympics. This travel to various major athletic events as well as my association with individual members of *Ramparts* staff has contributed greatly to my understanding of the role sport plays in contemporary American society.

Chapters 2, 3 and 5 were not written by me, and I wish to thank Homer Babbidge, Max Rafferty, and Dave Meggyesy for giving me permission to use the material in these chapters. Chapter 6 includes a number of articles written by sports writers for the school newspaper at the University of California at Berkeley, and I'm thankful to my friends, Lewis Leader, Randy Smyth, Tony Fogliani, and Jim Smith for permission to reprint their writings. And Chapter 11 probably never would have been written had I not received an invitation from Dr. Bryant Cratty, President of the North American Society for the Psychology of Sport and Physical Activity, to give a talk at his society's national meeting in the spring of 1970.

Libby Scheier, besides proofreading most of the manuscript, offered a number of excellent suggestions with regard to the actual content of the book. My parents, John and Lou Scott— even though in their sixties—rebuilt their lives anew during the period I was writing this book, and observing their courageous struggle was a constant source of inspiration.

Micki Scott offered many invaluable criticisms and suggestions while the book was in progress. Without Micki's almost daily assistance, as well as her love and understanding, this book might very well never have been completed.

Contents

PART II
Science and Sport

PART III
Sport, Education, and Society

Although interscholastic or intercollegiate athletics may be financed and otherwise controlled by the educational institution, the program should belong primarily to the students. It should reflect their interests, be geared to their capacities, and encourage widespread participation on the part of the student body. The more the program becomes a normal and meaningful part of student life, the greater its justification from the educational viewpoint.

HARRY A. SCOTT (1951)

In all schools, we should give much more time, money, and space for all the arts, and for developing physical strength, fitness, and skill. Sports, athletics, games are too important to be just for the varsity. In fact, our professionalizing of sports, down to the high school level, is the greatest enemy of general health and fitness that we have.

JOHN HOLT (1970)

PART I

THE TURMOIL
IN SPORT

Competitive sport is, in the eyes of its youthful critics, a part and parcel of the establishment. And without wanting to be an alarmist, let me say that I think that if the current undergraduate mood persists, intercollegiate athletics are going to be a target of criticism, disruption and protest. And if you'll stop to think about it for a moment, I think you'll agree that we are a prime target.

HOMER BABBIDGE, PRESIDENT
The University of Connecticut (1968)

1

One More Victim
of the NCAA

The case of Sylvester Hodges, a wrestler from Hayward State College in California, poignantly illustrates the reasons for much of the turmoil plaguing high school and college athletics in America today. Hodges enrolled at Hayward State College in 1966 after serving three years in the Air Force upon graduation from high school. He had been wrestling competitively since his junior year of high school, and by the time he was a senior at Hayward State, he was one of the outstanding college wrestlers in the country. In fact, he had become so skilled that he was undefeated his senior year and seemed a sure bet to win the NCAA college division championship, a goal toward which he had been striving for many years.

Hodges showed up at the 1969 NCAA college division wrestling tournament intent on winning the championship in his weight division. Sadly, he did not even get to wrestle in the tournament, let alone win the championship. He was barred from competing because he wore a mustache (see picture of Hodges on page 6).

NCAA officials in charge of wrestling had passed a rule earlier that year that prohibited anyone from competing in college wrestling who had facial hair below the middle of the ear. The rule had not been enforced during the season, but now, at the

3

championship tournament, the officials had decided to enforce it. Hodges and his coach, Dick Revenes, pointed out to the NCAA officials how he had worn this same mustache while wrestling in the Armed Services for three years without incident. They also explained that wrestlers in the Olympic Games and other international competitions regularly compete with mustaches, beards, and long hair. But the efforts of Hodges and his coach to reason with the NCAA officials proved futile, and he was not allowed to compete.

I first met Sylvester Hodges approximately one year after he was barred from competing in the NCAA tournament when I invited him to talk about this experience with students in a course I was teaching at the University of California at Berkeley entitled Intercollegiate Athletics and Higher Education: A Socio-Psychological Evaluation. One of the aims of the course was to examine the personal and social reasons for the increasing discontent among college athletes throughout the country. The following is the talk Hodges gave to the class.

I've been wrestling for approximately eleven years. I first started wrestling in the eleventh grade at McClymonds High School in Oakland. I wasn't very good at the time. I took third in the city championship my junior year and second when I was a senior.

I joined the Air Force after I graduated from high school and worked as an aircraft missile electrician. I met one of the most famous wrestlers around while I was in the Air Force. His name is Russell Camilleri, and he has been to the Olympics a few times. Whenever he gets ready to go, he goes. He's that good.

I met Russell one day when I was out running. I like to run. I just like to get out and run. This is my religion. A lot of people have to go to church to get that feeling; I get it from just going out and running. And I run, and run, and run. I feel good when I finish. I was out running and he saw me and said he wanted to run along with me. Well, I told him if he could keep up, he could run. So I ran him, and I ran him so good that I left him and came back for him. He asked me to join the wrestling team, and I did. I guess he figured a guy in my condition would be a pretty good wrestler even if he didn't know too much. So I joined the Air Force team, and that's where I learned a lot about wrestling, mostly from Russell.

I participated on the Air Force wrestling team for three years and really began to develop my skills. After I was discharged from the Air Force, I got stimulated by an old wrestling coach from high school to go back to college. And that is what I did; I went back to school. Wrestling, the way I did it, helped me to stay in college because I enjoyed it. If I didn't enjoy it and it became work, I never would have continued. But I enjoyed it. I developed my skills by practicing with many different people. I traveled everywhere I could find people who knew something about wrestling, and wrestled against them.

I began wrestling for Cal State a few years ago. I'm a pretty good wrestler now; I win most of the time. When I lose, I chalk that one up as a win next time and I go back around and I get it. I found out you can beat anybody you want to beat if you're willing to put the work into doing it. I use this philosophy in every part of my life. I believe I can accomplish anything I want to if I'm willing to do the required work.

I've traveled all over the United States wrestling, and I've looked like this ever since the eleventh grade when I first grew my mustache. It's never been any bigger than this. I like it just like it is.

I try to keep up on the latest rules on wrestling so that I can use them to my advantage. One day last year I was thumbing through the rule book and discovered they had a new rule saying you had to be clean shaven. And that's as far as it went—it simply said clean shaven. So, because I'm interested in wrestling and I intend to be a coach besides a physical education instructor, I thought I'd write to them and try to find out what they meant by clean shaven. That's kind of a vague statement, and I had heard that some coaches and referees in Los Angeles were interpreting it to mean no facial hair at all—no hair below the ear lobes.

I wrote the NCAA rules committee, but they didn't answer me directly. They put their response to my letter in the *Wrestling*

Sylvester Hodges, champion wrestler at Hayward State College. This picture was taken only a few days before NCAA officials barred Hodges from wrestling in the NCAA Championship tournament because of his mustache. Your eyes are not failing you; Hodges mustache really was that minuscule (*Audio-Visual Services, California State College, Hayward*).

News. I read it there first, and then about a month later I got a letter from them stating that clean shaven meant no hair below the ear lobes. I looked for some justification for this ruling, but could find none in their article. Now you have to understand that I'm a person who doesn't do anything until I find out *why*. So I was curious to know the reason for this rule, and I asked a lot of different people who were supposed to know why, and nobody knew why. Their only response was, " 'Cause we said so, that's why."

I've been wrestling for a lot of years now, and I know quite a bit about wrestling. I figure only two people know more than me about wrestling, and I don't know them yet. I really feel that confident. If it's conceit, well, I got a little bit of it, I guess. So I was trying to figure out for myself why they would make that rule, because I had faith in the people. I said maybe it's a safety hazard. I figured out all angles and decided it couldn't be a safety hazard. You couldn't use this one, not my mustache, to hurt someone. Even the girls don't complain when I kiss them, so I knew I couldn't hurt anybody or tickle them. So it wasn't for safety. Some people said maybe it could cause you to catch germs if you get cut in the face. To them I simply said, "What if you get cut in the head? You've got hair on your head." So it didn't make sense that way. No matter what way I looked at it, the rule didn't make any sense, so I decided I wasn't going to shave off my mustache.

I went in and told the coach because I didn't know how he felt. Dr. Revenes is the coach. He's a heavy, as they refer to the guys that got it; he's really heavy. I showed him the rule and told him I wasn't going to cut my mustache off and that I felt strong about it. I felt they were infringing on my rights because there was no reason they could show me for the rule. If anyone here tonight can give me a good reason pertaining to my sport why I should cut it off, I will. If you have a razor, I'll do it right now, as long as you can give me a good reason.

Anyway, I told the coach how I felt. I thought he might be the old-fashioned kind of coach that tries to tell you what to do. But he didn't. Instead, he asked me, "Do you really feel strongly about it?" I told him I did. He then asked me, "Do you feel strongly enough that under any circumstances you wouldn't shave it off?" I said, "That's the way I feel." He said, "Some people will say that, but when it comes down to a showdown, they'll back down." So I assured him I really felt this way about it. I had had it ever since the eleventh grade, even through the service. They made everybody shave in the service, but they didn't bother me. He said that as long as that was how I felt, he would go all the way with me. Like I told you, he's a heavy—a good man.

Coach Revenes and I went and talked to Dr. Morford, the head of the physical education department. I didn't know him too well then. We called him "god." He walked around with his head in the air, and he had that cold, monster look on his face. He didn't smile too often. You didn't want to speak to him. So everybody called him "god." We went in to see "god," and we explained to him how I felt and what the rule was. I thought that this was where I would get it, especially since I was a P.E. major. But I was willing to give up my career in school and a degree before I would shave off my mustache because of a senseless rule. Whatever Dr. Morford was going to run down to me, I didn't care. He was either with me, or that was it—I'd face up to whatever I had to. Well, we talked to "god," and I found out that he was all right. His ideas on athletics and athletes are really fine. He said he'd back me all the way, even if it cost him his job.

I had Dr. Morford's support, and I had the support of my coach. But, believe it or not, I didn't need their support. I did appreciate it though. I didn't need it because, regardless of whose support I had, I was going to go as far as I could with my mustache, and when I couldn't go any further, I was going to leave with my mustache. With their backing, I went all the way in the Far Western Conference. I was winning. I was undefeated, and I was just beating everybody. They knew I was bad. A lot of the coaches didn't want me around because that was the only way their guys could make it in my division—if I wasn't around. And I think some of them, solely on this ground, wanted me barred. At least this is what a lot of the athletes from other schools told me. Most of the coaches didn't even know I had a mustache. They've talked to me, I've seen them around at many different tournaments, and most of them never knew I had a mustache until the publicity began in the papers.

Anyway, we decided to go. The Far Western Conference wasn't going to let me wrestle to qualify for the NCAA until we took a survey and found that we had more people in favor of me going than were against me. I went to the Far Western Conference finals, and I wanted to make sure I went to the NCAA, so I wrapped it up good. I wasn't even scored against—not a point against me in the entire tournament. I was really ready, for I wanted to go all the way. I wanted to win an NCAA championship, something that had been my goal for eleven years.

I arrived in San Luis Obispo for the NCAA finals undefeated. I was all dressed and ready to go out to the mats when the coach from San Luis Obispo came up to me—he knew me because I'd whipped some of his guys earlier in the year—and said, "You're not going to wrestle today." I said, "I'm not, huh?" He said, "No. Unless you cut that thing off." I asked him, "What thing?" because he had me worried. I wasn't sure just what thing he wanted me to cut off. I told him I didn't want to talk to him anymore after he made that smart remark. I just walked away. If I had said something, the next thing would have been violence—my people believe in violence. And I would have hit him because I think he was trying to pick on me in a way he shouldn't have been.

There were eight to ten athletes at the NCAA's who were black that had mustaches and about three white athletes also had mustaches. Some of these blacks were from Howard University, a few were from a couple of other schools, and one was my closest buddy—we'd been wrestling together for about eight years—from San Francisco State. Guess what they did? Just like that, cut them off. Some of them dry shaved their mustaches off. They all told me, "Oh, I'm going right along with you," but when it came down to the wire, they had that razor because their coaches told them, "You better cut it off." One coach told his guy, "You better cut it off or there ain't no sense in your coming back to school."

I stood there all dressed and prepared—ready to go. They

called my name, and I walked out to the mat. I knew that
according to the rule book, they couldn't disqualify me until I
got out there on the mat. You should have seen them! The
referee didn't know I had a mustache. I'm walking out on the
mat and he's ready to start the match, and you should have
seen the coaches run. "Hey, hey, who's going to stop him? Who's
going to stop him?" They were running around trying to find
the tournament director to get him to stop me from wrestling.
The referee was ready to make things go on just like they should
have been going.

The guy I was going to wrestle was a guy I'd been wanting to
wrestle for years. He was from Mankato, Minnesota. They think
they're the best in wrestling, and they don't know that anyone
else from any other part of the country can be just as good with
a lot of effort. Plus, I had already spotted his weakness. He had
a taped-up shoulder that was suppose to have been hidden, but
I could see the tape peeking out over his shoulder blade. I was
after it. You don't come out on the mat with me unless you're
ready. If you call yourself ready with a bum shoulder, then I'm
ready too, and I'll get it. I was ready to whip this cat—he was
going to be the first off the list—and then I was going to go on
and do my thing with the other guys.

I was standing there looking at my opponent and he was
standing there looking at me. The referee was about ready to
give the signal to wrestle when this guy came running out to
stop me from wrestling. He said, "Hey, this guy can't wrestle; he
has a mustache." The referee looked at me—he was an old
friend of mine, I knew him from all my years of wrestling—and
he said, "Hodges, I can't let you wrestle. We'll give you two
minutes to cut your mustache off." I said, "Don't give me no time
because I'm not going to cut it off." He said, "Well, officially we
have to give it to you." So there I stood before all those thousands of people in the stands. We had to stand out there for two
minutes.

One of the coaches came over and told me, "Why don't you
cut it off? You're at the top; you can go all the way this year;
you can really make the top in wrestling." And I felt I could. I
felt nothing could stop me because I had what they call that

cocky feeling—when you're feeling nobody can touch you. That's when most athletes know they're at their peak. Well, I had that feeling and I knew it, and I knew that coach realized I had the ability to go all the way. He said, "Why don't you. You could always grow it back." I said, "Yes. But there are certain things you can't acquire back once you lose them, and one of them is your self-respect."

So I stood there and the time ran out; the cat came out—I don't know if he thought I was going to hit him or what—he walked up and said, "You've got to leave the mat," and he stepped three steps back from me. He said, "You can't wrestle." I said, "All right then," and I shook my opponent's hand and said, "You sure are lucky!" and I walked off the mat and just walked out.

But to me that was the moment—those two minutes that they gave me to shave my mustache off or leave—to me that was the deciding moment that meant something to me in life more than just not shaving off a little mustache. Because usually once a year I'll trim it down real low where you can't hardly see it anyway, and possibly I could even shave it off once a year—it wouldn't matter that much under any other circumstances. But for someone who doesn't have a bit, not a damn bit of business to do with some part of my body to tell me to do something with it—I just couldn't see doing it.

Immediately after the NCAA championship tournament in which Hodges was barred from competing, 510 college wrestling coaches were polled on how they felt about the "no-hair" rule. Many athletes, educators, and sport fans throughout the country were confident that once NCAA officials and coaches realized this regulation had resulted in the barring of an individual like Hodges, they would quickly vote to repeal it. However, the results of the poll showed that over 490 of the coaches voted in favor of retaining the "no-hair" rule. Not surprisingly, given this kind of support from the coaches, NCAA officials have retained the rule, and individuals with "facial hair below the middle of the ear lobe" are still not allowed to compete.

The response of Jim Smith, the head wrestling coach at the

University of Washington, reveals the callous, "law and order" stance most wrestling coaches have taken on the Hodges case. I was speaking before a group of educators at the University of Washington and Smith happened to be at the meeting. In explaining the Hodges affair to the group, I suggested that a mistake was made in barring him from competing. Smith immediately commented, "The ONLY MISTAKE made was that Hodges wasn't stopped from competing long before the NCAA Championship. He shouldn't have been allowed to participate in any meets wearing a mustache." As Dr. Robert Morford, the chairman of the Department of Physical Education at Hayward State College, aptly points out, "The barring of Sylvester certainly doesn't seem to have had any noticeable effect on most coaches."[1]

1. Hodges has not allowed his treatment by the NCAA to get him down, and he is presently working as a physical education teacher and coach at a California high school. Though he has good reason to be bitter and cynical, he is not. He is still struggling to bring about needed changes in the athletic world, and he feels better equipped for this struggle now that he is no longer naïve about the true nature of those individuals who run athletics in America. It is through the mature, long-term commitment of individuals like Sylvester Hodges and his fine coach, Dick Revenes, that constructive changes will eventually occur in the athletic programs of our schools and colleges.

2

Interscholastic Athletics:
the Gathering Storm

BY MAX RAFFERTY

One of my primary goals in writing this book was to shed some light on the reasons for the turmoil plaguing American high school and college athletics. It is with this purpose in mind that I have included the following text of a speech delivered to the 1969 California State Conference of Athletic Directors by Max Rafferty, former California State Superintendent of Public Instruction. Most educators react to Rafferty with emotions ranging from amusement to dismay. But athletic directors and coaches, such as those assembled in San Francisco at the state conference where he gave this speech, enthusiastically embrace him and his ideas. Those present at the conference gave him a tumultuous, standing ovation at the conclusion of this talk. They view Rafferty with admiration and respect, for he articulates the feelings and attitudes they have but cannot adequately express.

Those of you who are at first amused by Rafferty's remarks should remember that what he expresses is the dominant philosophy in American athletics, one which most high school and college athletes encounter daily in varying degrees. But as Bob Dylan says, "The Times They Are A-Changin'," and an ever increasing number of athletes, and even some of their coaches, are beginning to rebel against the approach to athletics espoused by Rafferty. The athletic accomplishments of these athletes and coaches are empirical evidence that they are no less dedicated or disciplined than those Rafferty admires. Athletics in America have for so long functioned in a quasi-militaristic, authoritarian manner guided by values of manliness, agressiveness, and super-competitiveness, that Rafferty—quite understandably—assumes that anyone who does not agree with this approach to sport could not possibly love or enjoy athletics.

Just in case you don't know it, you fellows are under the gun these days. More importantly, so is everything you stand for.

There are two great national institutions which simply cannot tolerate either internal dissension or external interference: our armed forces, and our interscholastic sports program. Both are of necessity benevolent dictatorships because by their very nature they cannot be otherwise. A combat squad which has to sit down and poll its members before it reacts to an emergency has had it, and so has a football team which lets its opponents tell it whom to start in next Saturday's game.

Ridiculous, you say? Yet both these ridiculous things are happening, or threatening to happen. If you're up on the news at all, you're familiar with the problem the army and marines have been having in recent months with men who go on hunger strikes and who refuse to obey orders on the battlefield. You should be even more familiar with what's happening on the athletic field.

To pinpoint what I'm talking about, let's look at a couple of examples of how sports are being pressured and used to do things they were never intended to do at all.

First, let's look at the "Great Pumpkin," as his Oregon State players call coach Dee Andros. Andros is of Greek descent, like Spiro Agnew, and he's just as good at football coaching as Agnew is at pointing out the faults of the news media, which is pretty darned good. Unfortunately, Andros has a problem.

For 21 years, he's had an invariable rule that his gridiron gladiators look the part. His squads have always enjoyed sky-high morale, much of it due to the fact that the players are encouraged to regard the team as more important than the individual player, and the combined effort more valuable than the heroics of the loner. Long ago, the coach banned the freak out as an acceptable avocation for Oregon State footballers.

Dr. Max Rafferty, former State Superintendent of Public Instruction in California. Rafferty began his career in education as a high school football coach and compiled an outstanding winning record over a five-year period. He still regularly speaks out on athletics: "There are two great national institutions which simply cannot tolerate either internal dissension or external interference: our armed forces, and our interscholastic sports programs. Both are of necessity benevolent dictatorships. . ." (*Wide World Photos*).

In other words: if you want to play for me, fellows, no girlish necklaces and cutesy medallions, no Iroquois scalplocks, no hair-mattress beards, and no Fu Manchu moustaches. You can sport these execrable excrescences and still go to Oregon State, but you can't massage your egos thus publicly and still play football for Dee Andros. Period.

At least right up until last spring it was "period." The Battling Beavers of OSU won a lot more games than they lost, and what's far more important they managed to win them while looking like decent human beings instead of like fugitives from a Barnum and Bailey side show.

They were shaven, they were shorn, they wore men's clothing rather than feminine fripperies, and they actually looked as though they bathed once in a while. In short, the varsity players stood out like lighthouses alongside the campus activists, many of whom look and smell as though they had recently emerged from ten years' solitary confinement on Devil's Island.

And this last is undoubtedly what triggered Andros' current crisis.

It seems that some hulking lout on his squad decided to defy the team's personal appearance rules and to sprout a luxuriant thicket of facial foliage which viewed under his helmet and behind his face-guard made him virtually indistinguishable from a gorilla. The coach said: "Shave it off or shove off." The player refused and appealed to Oregon State's president on the grounds that his civil rights were being violated.

Instead of backing up his coach and telling the hairy one to get lost, the OSU prexy appointed a Commission on Human Rights to investigate the coach, thus firmly establishing the president's credentials as an even bigger ass than the exhibitionist player. The commission dutifully censured Andros for showing "insufficient sensitivity to the sacred right of adolescent showoffs to break coaching rules."

Kindly note at this juncture that nobody at Oregon State is compelled to play football. Note also that the coach's rules have been part of his winning formula for more than two decades, and are well-known to almost everyone in the state of Oregon. The alternative is laughably simple, and it's true on every campus and for every sport: if you don't like the rules, don't go out for the sport.

Now just where does the decision by the Human Rights Commission's driveling academicians leave Dee Andros? What's the future of a coach whose players now know he may be road-blocked and face-slapped by some ad hoc committee every time he tells them to do something they don't want to do?

I can't think of a better way to destroy a fine football team, can you? Or a fine coach, for that matter. But maybe that's the whole idea.

Up to now, I've never known that exquisite sensitivity to a player's pampered ego was one of the prerequisites for a good coach. I've always thought a coach's job was to make men out of wet-behind-the-ears boys.

Can you imagine the expression on gruff old Knute Rockne's face if some cap-and-gowned buffoon had called him "insufficiently sensitive"?

Second, along the same lines but with even more unsavory overtones, there's the recent case of Stanford University's foray into the unlovely field of religious persecution, with athletics playing the role of unwilling patsy. It seems that Stanford recently and scathingly severed athletic relations with Brigham Young University because of one of the fundamental tenets of the Mormon faith: that the descendants of Canaan are ineligible by Old Testament mandate to hold the highest offices in the Church. Inasmuch as those descendants are held by long tradition to be black, Negroes are thus disqualified from taking their place as priests and bishops of the Mormon faith.

Result: not many Negroes are Mormons. Additional result: no black football players at BYU. So Stanford joins several other colleges in a kind of anti-Mormon Coalition which is boycotting the Utah school until it mends its allegedly wicked ways, and they are presently writing unctuous letters to each other congratulating themselves on their own virtue.

So far, so good. But let's carry the story one step further. The Coalition isn't trying merely to get Brigham Young to put Negroes on its football team. If that's all there were to it, you wouldn't be hearing a single squawk out of me, because I firmly believe that all education, and athletics in particular, should be completely integrated and conspicuously multiracial. Unlike some southern schools which the Coalition somehow didn't get around to denouncing, though, BYU is perfectly willing to do just that, has in fact featured black athletes on some of its past teams, and is currently looking for some more. No, what the Coalition is really demanding is something far, far, different. It's that the Church of the Latter Day Saints repudiate part of its established dogma, given to it a century and a half ago, according to its scriptures by divine revelation.

Now this is quite another matter. What on earth would you do if you were athletic director in a case of this kind? Brigham Young University, you see, is a Church school. Its policies must perforce reflect the teachings of that Church, and cannot contravene them. In effect, the Church *is* the school, and vice versa. So the Coalition isn't just demanding that a sister school simply change an athletic policy; it's conducting an organized boycott of a deeply held theological belief, and this sort of religious persecution in the final third of the twentieth century is absolutely intolerable.

It's as though the Coalition were to boycott an Episcopalian college because we Episcopalians don't permit females to be bishops, or to put pressure on a Jewish university because Judaism won't allow ham sandwich-munchers to become rabbis. I don't happen to agree at all that the color of a man's skin should keep him from becoming a priest, a bishop, or a pope, for that matter, in any church. But I don't happen to be a Mormon, and what the Mormons devoutly believe is simply none of my Episcopalian business. Neither is it the business of athletics in general, or the Coalition in particular.

So long as BYU keeps up its academic standards, behaves itself properly on the playing field, and opens its classrooms and its athletic teams alike to all who qualify for entrance regardless of color or race, it's as outrageous for the Coalition to use athletics to interfere with a church's right to practice its own faith as it was for the jolly jesters of the Third Reich to interfere with the German Jews' right to practice theirs. The BYU students, incidentally, have an impeccable record in regard to the criteria I've just listed, and what's more, stayed soberly in class last year while the Stanfordites were bloodily occupying administration buildings and raising hell generally.

Ah, well. Football is supposed to teach players sportsmanship, fellowship, and fair play. I'm sure BYU can find other schools beside those of the Coalition to supply this desired mixture, and which won't also expose its players to the added and unwelcome ingredient of religious intolerance.

My purpose in bringing these incidents before you tonight is simply to remind you of their increasing frequency. At San Jose, Wyoming, Washington, and a dozen other distracted colleges, players have challenged their coaches, walked out on their own teams, and boycotted their own schools, all in the name of some social, economic, or political grievance which the sport in question had never had anything to do with and with which it was never set up to cope.

As athletic directors, you're up against more than just a challenge to your authority or that of your coaches, a temporary road-block in the path of bigger and better athletic competition. What's facing you in the very near future is the possible elimination of school sports altogether, if only because sports as we know them cannot survive their transformation into a mere tool of various activist groups with their own non-athletic axes to grind.

It's ironical, in fact, that those who hate athletics the most are the ones currently trying to use athletics for their own ends. These, of course, are the "Let's-give-aid-and-comfort-to-the-Communists" agitators, the hairy, loud-mouthed freaks of both sexes who infest our campuses today like so many unbathed boll weevils. The activists and the pseudo-intellectuals have created a myth—a kind of anti-athlete cartoon caricature which I'd like to analyze briefly.

The stereotype is that of the muscle-bound and moronic athlete. Of late he has receipted for so many "avant garde" jokes that he has become a permanent cliché, like the college widow and the absent-minded professor. Yet when one puts the myth of the jug-headed, oafish muscle-man under the cold light of logical analysis, it doesn't hold up worth a nickel.

The beard-and-sandal set claims the athlete is stupid. Yet in every high school where I've ever worked, the grade-point average of the varsity players was higher than that of the student body as a whole.

The lank-haired leaders of our campus revolutionists sneer at the varsity letterman for his allegedly juvenile enthusiasms and his willingness to die for dear old Rutgers. But they themselves are quite openly and ardently guilty of enthusiasms for such strange causes as raising bail money for Mario Savio and paying Joan Baez's taxes, and they seem ready to die at a moment's notice for a smile from Kosygin or even for the slightest relaxation of the built-in scowl on the face of Mao-Tse-Tung. By comparison, dying for Rutgers has its points.

Their intellectual vials of wrath are constantly overflowing onto the hapless head of the athlete because of his hopeless Philistinism and his alleged inability to communicate with his peers save in monosyllabic grunts. Yet the halls of Congress and the board rooms of giant industrial complexes are alike populated by a striking number of ex-athletes who seem to have no difficulty whatever in communicating. And the Philistine mentality of such former contenders on the playing fields as Douglas MacArthur, John F. Kennedy, and Justice Byron "Whizzer" White may be left safely for history to judge.

As another football season ends and another basketball season begins, I have to confess a lifelong fondness for the amateur athlete. Over the past thirty years, eight of which were spent as a high school coach and athletic director, I've seen a remarkable number of athletes fighting and even dying for their country, and remarkably few of them ending up in jail or taking the Fifth Amendment before a Congressional investigating committee. They seem to be conspicuously absent, too, from Communist-inspired demonstrations and Filthy Speech Movements.

They are, in short, above-average, decent, reasonably patriotic Americans. Maybe that's why they're under increasing attack from the kooks, the crum-bums, and Commies.

I'm not too worried about the outcome. The love of clean, competitive sports is too deeply imbedded in the American matrix, too much a part of the warp and woof of our free people, ever to surrender to the burning-eyed, bearded draft-card-burners who hate and envy the athlete because he is something they can never be—a *man*.

Our greatest soldier-statesman of the twentieth century once had this to say about athletics and the men who follow its rigorous and rewarding discipline: "Upon the fields of friendly strife are sown the seeds which, on other days, on other fields, will bear the seeds of victory."

As athletic directors, you have a decision to make. The college syndrome I have noted and documented in this brief talk is spreading into American high schools even as we meet together tonight. Your choice is simple: you can back up your coaches' authority to do with their teams what coaches have done for the last hundred years, or you can play a cowardly game of patty-cake with the activists and watch your sports program go down the drain with your own jobs going right along with it.

I didn't come here tonight to make you feel good, but rather to do two things: warn you, and promise to help. Little enough of idealism and faith and cheerful willingness to fight on steadfastly for the right remains to us Americans in these, the Sick Sixties. Interscholastic sports, rising surprisingly and increasingly above their age-old status as mere games, serve today as the staunch custodians of these treasured concepts out of our great past.

If you elect to cop out on all this and to let your teams be used for their own sinister purposes by those who are the enemies of all athletics, you will deserve exactly what you will get, and you will receive no sympathy from me. But if you decide to stand your ground and fight for the future of American sports against those who would destroy everything you've worked for all your lives, then indeed you will have formidable allies: my own Department; the vast majority of our state legislators; above all, the millions of Californians who love athletics and who believe with all their hearts that it symbolizes the clean, bright, fighting spirit which is America herself.

A tough job, this one which I am urging upon you? You bet. But you are tough men, or should be. These are rugged times, and we need rugged men to stand up to them. My own job, over the years, has not been exactly a bed of roses. All you and I can do is to lower our heads and do our level best, keeping the goals of our great profession constantly before our mind's eye, disregarding as best we can the barrage of the opposition, striving to keep our feet despite the shell holes and the booby traps, satisfied if the end of each day finds us a little closer to our hearts' desire.

When I grow tired, as I occasionally do—when I get discouraged, as once in a while happens—when the slings and arrows of our common enemies get to me, as they do now and then—there is one never-failing source of inspiration upon which I learned long ago to rely, and which always sends me back into the fray with renewed strength and a stout heart.

It's a very simple thing. I merely close my eyes and call up from the depths of memory my old teams—the myriad faces which have passed before me for so many years—the bright, fresh, questing faces of the kids with whom I lived and worked for so long. Those strong, eager boys, so willing to learn, so wrapped up in the joy of playing the game for the game's sake, the only way it ever should be played. I look back upon the long parade of faces, and in my mind I see the countless more whom in reality I will never get to see—the youngsters of California—your own teams—thronging in their untold thousands from the redwood country of the north to the great desert which lies along our southern border.

And suddenly it's all worth while. What men ever had more children than you and I to work for, to hope for, to live for? More than two million boys—the joy, the hope, the whole future of our state. It's a family worth fighting for.

I recommend it to you.

3

Athletics and the
American Dream

BY HOMER BABBIDGE

The following is the text of a speech delivered by Homer D. Babbidge, president of the University of Connecticut, to the National Association of Collegiate Athletic Directors in Cleveland, Ohio, on June 24, 1968. In the tempered tone of a university president, Dr. Babbidge told the assembled athletic directors that before long they should expect to come under attack from student activists unless they eliminate the hypocrisy and exploitation extant in many of their programs. He encouraged them to give a participant orientation to their athletic programs and discussed some of the specific steps the University of Connecticut was taking to develop an educationally relevant athletic program.

Though Dr. Babbidge offered many excellent suggestions for improving intercollegiate athletics, perhaps the most significant aspect of his address was the reaction to it on the part of the athletic directors. Though he exhibited great restraint throughout his talk in an effort not to unduly antagonize them, most of the athletic directors reacted to his speech as if they had just had the Communist Manifesto read to them by Fidel Castro! I talked with J. D. Morgan, the well-known athletic director of UCLA, about Dr. Babbidge's speech almost a year later. Straining to suppress his anger over the fact that such a speech was even allowed to be given at their national meeting, Morgan at first refused to comment directly on Dr. Babbidge's talk. However, he did sardonically mention, "University presidents seem to be having enough trouble running the rest of the university. I think they'd do well to keep their noses out of college athletics."

Dr. Babbidge correctly prophesied the current assault on intercollegiate athletics by student activists, but what he did not foresee was that athletes, always a docile group when it came to protest activity, would join this assault. The fundamental difference between the contemporary movement to humanize college athletics and those of the past is that today athletes are often in the forefront of the movement.

A status report on American higher education today, just has to be a discussion of student unrest; and I must, therefore, impose upon you *yet one more* amateur analysis of what makes today's student behave as he does.

It's a dangerous business. Just a few weeks ago, President Pusey of Harvard allowed himself to be quoted as saying he thought student demonstrations were tapering off. That same day, the Columbia University protestors swung into action.

It's always dangerous to undertake publicly an analysis of current developments. It's probably best left to the syndicated columnist. And for that reason I'm going to refrain from trying to analyze the dramatic expressions of student unrest that have populated the press in recent weeks, and talk instead about what I perceive to be more profound currents of student sentiment. But it's worth looking at the trouble spots to get a line on those currents.

The principal concerns of student activists today appear to center around three storm centers: The Viet Nam War, race relations and their own educations. They're saying, in effect, that the adult world has botched all three. Not all students feel equally strongly about all three matters, and a few aren't concerned about any of them. But it's pretty hard to find students— in a university, at least—who don't fault adult society on at least one of these major issues. And having found adults culpable in one area, the student will listen sympathetically to those who accuse us of failure in another. And thus it is that loosely formed alliances of youthful critics and skeptics keep adults on the go all along an extended "defense perimeter."

Many thoughtful adults realize, deep down in their hearts, that our young critics are—in some degree, difficult to measure— justified in their criticisms. Take the three central issues: neither hawks or doves nor self-styled owls can express gratification with our posture in Viet Nam; certainly no reasonable man can deny the crisis in race relations; and I, for one, am prepared to admit to grievous shortcomings in our educational efforts.

Our adult view of these issues is, of course, different from that of the young people. We are more conscious than they of the progress that has been recorded in some of these areas; we are familiar from personal experience, with the obstacles to progress; we are conscious of our own personal efforts to resolve these issues, and many of us do not feel any personal sense of guilt about our own records. By standards that once prevailed, some adults have records of aggressive and positive leadership. They are understandably pained by the accusation that they have failed, or have not really tried.

As in all human affairs, there are those who see the glass half full and those who see it half empty. Both observations may be objectively accurate, but it's pretty hard for either to persuade the other to his point of view.

But I think we adults have to remind ourselves that ours is a society that is dedicated to something more than the half-filled glass. Teddy Roosevelt would hardly have campaigned for a "half-full dinner pail." The proudest features of our national charter dedicate us to a fullness of human realization that ought always to be our goal.

And it's our tendency, when our attention is directed to the emptiness of the glass, to reply by pointing to its fullness. That gets us in dutch with young people. Our failure to handle their criticisms to their satisfaction is what leads to youthful cynicism about adults and the established order.

I am definitely *not* saying that we should overlook the progress of our past. Indeed, I find odious the tendency among some to denigrate our national past. A sense of progress toward our national goals is essential to the maintenance of morale in our further efforts to achieve them. We need to study the progress of the past, not to take comfort in it or to support a sense of complacency; but to reassure ourselves that the aims and goals of our society have proven viable over time—that what we are determined to do tomorrow is not only desirable but possible.

But what we must not do, it seems to me, is to deny that the glass is still less than full. We must try and make it clear to young people, first of all, that we share with them a desire to see that fullness of human dignity that is their passionate goal; and secondly that we are prepared, old and tired as some of us may be, to work still harder toward that goal.

I say this out of a firm conviction that the "over 30 crowd" really does care—that it still subscribes to the American Dream. But the younger generation apparently does not believe it. And the reason they don't is that we adults present ourselves to them as a kind of "drag"—a force that tends to stifle and slow down the pace and tempo of progress.

Now, at this point, let me be entirely candid. Adults are, inevitably, I think, just such a force in society. Not, however, just because they have become fat or rich or lazy or captives of an establishment; not because they are "middle class." (A favorite charge of our critics.)

Adults are a drag on youthful enthusiasm because they believe that order is the second law of nature. They believe that optimum human fulfillment is possible only in a society governed by laws. They believe that lasting human progress is dependent upon stable institutions. They believe that a structured society is necessary to reconcile the constructive and destructive forces—the good and the evil—that exists in all men. They believe that in a society so ordered and structured reason will win out over unreason.

And since these are profound convictions among adults, they are not going to disappear. Nor, in my judgment, should they. They constitute the very foundations of civilization, as we have known it.

But young people misread these convictions, and not entirely without justification. I am afraid it's true that these important convictions are used by some adults to justify and defend the status quo, and to enforce an unwarranted conformity.

To believe in law and order is no excuse for tolerating unjust laws. To believe in the importance of stability is no justification for oppression. To believe in institutions is no grounds for depersonalizing them, or draining them of a quality of responsiveness.

The real test for the adult world—indeed, the real test for our society—is to demonstrate convincingly that our dedication is to ideals and principles, and not to what we can, in a selfish sense, derive from lip service to those ideals and principles as they currently apply.

The adult who works actively to bring our laws more closely into harmony with true justice will be trusted when he says he believes in a government of laws, and he will have taken a long step in demonstrating the validity of that belief. And the educator who seeks to make his institution more responsive and relevant to the needs of today's learners, will have made a convincing case that institutions should survive as a mechanism for the achievement of cultural and social goals.

If we can persuade youth that we share their dedication to progress, that we are agreeable to change even when it hurts us personally, then the debate narrows. Then and only then can we get in a few licks in support of the principles of political order that are to us so essential.

I told you I was going to talk with you today about the younger generation, but you see I've talked more about the older generation. But I honestly believe that the thinking of our younger generation is mainly influenced by their response to us—to what we are or appear to be. And we have a bad image.

But let me say a few words more directly about the younger generation. And let me say it first by observing that the best kept secret of this rising generation is that it is essentially idealistic. To be sure, it's a generation that has a great many other characteristics, some of which tend to obscure or camouflage this basic idealism. This is, as we all know, a generation that has not known war or depression. To it, World War II is as remote as the War to Save Democracy was to their parents. And to them, serious economic deprivation is about as remote as were the "poor, starving Belgians" about whom their *grandparents* spoke in an effort to get their *parents* to finish their spinach.

And it's not only that this generation has no first-hand exposure to war or poverty. Their sense of peaceful abundance is compounded by the fact that they are the children of parents who *have* seen famine and war—and who have, by and large, reacted by smothering their own children with the things that they themselves were denied. The excesses of affluence are seen not so much in the way in which adults indulge *their* wants as in the manner in which they over-indulge the whims of their children. Parents today are doing for their children not only more than they need or more than is probably good for them; they are actually urging on their children things they don't even want.

And so we should not be surprised that a rising generation of young people should seem at times to expect a lot, take a lot for granted. Indeed, the wonder is that any homely virtues survive in them at all. And yet they do.

How can it be that this spoiled generation can flock to the Peace Corps as bees to the comb? How can they bring themselves to trade the college convertible in on a job that pays 20 cents an hour without so much as a coffee break? Is it that they simply rebel instinctively at the affluence of their surroundings? Has their forced over-indulgence given them a spiritual belly ache?

Or do they find something lacking in the "adult" society that is being urged upon them?

Whatever the cause, I am prepared to testify on the basis of personal experience that this rising generation is looking for something that we adults make it inordinately hard for them to find. And that something is purpose and meaning that transcend self.

You can see evidence of this, if you'll look for it, in the selfless activities they enjoy. This losing of self in efforts to help others, I'm convinced, is going on quietly and without dramatics or fanfare on college and university campuses across the country, and should not be judged alone by the widely advertised incidents of recent weeks.

Even in their avowed political views, today's students espouse what they take to be ideals. They tend to polarize as conservatives or liberal, expressing their doubts about conventional middle-of-the-road-ism. They think they see in conventionality and moderation too much compromise, too much temporizing, too much timidity.

Today's students rally, as have idealists for a century, to the cry of Horace Mann: "Ally thyself with some great cause." And as misguided as we adults may regard either (or both) of these political extremes, we do well to acknowledge that their appeal to youngsters is idealistic—impractical and unwise, perhaps; but idealistic beyond doubt.

Now, I persist in labelling this generation as idealistic, and I ought at least to acknowledge that it's an unwelcome label. Ask a college student today if he's an idealist, and he'll give you a pretty fair imitation of a look of scorn and contempt. He'll ask you if you're nuts or something. For the rising generation has mastered the lingo of adult cynics, having discovered that it's an effective way of discouraging nosey adults from prying too much. And one of the reasons they don't want adults prying is that they fear adults do not understand their profound, private cravings—their idealism.

And, as I've tried to suggest, we adults have given them ample reason to think we don't understand youthful idealism. Where, but from us, have they learned that it's smart to be cynical, materialistic, selfish, compromising?

And where, but from us, can they get opposite counsel? Our adult society has it within its power to sustain and encourage the idealism of youth, though I have to concede we would have to resolve some major dilemmas in the adult world in order to do so.

Now, you may properly ask, what do the war in Viet Nam, the racial crisis, and shortcomings in the academic process have to do with us? What does all this student unrest have to do with us, in intercollegiate athletics? Our teams and our players, by and large, are the guys in the white hats—they keep their hair cut short, they're clean, they're orderly, aware of the importance of law and order and discipline. The students and

others who come to watch us play are the people who respect
tradition and institutional pride and a lot of other time-proven
values. We represent, you may say, a common force in modern
undergraduate society.

And that's precisely what constitutes our problem in intercollegiate athletics. Competitive sport is, in the eyes of its youthful
critics, a part and parcel of the establishment. And without
wanting to be an alarmist, let me say that I think that if the
current undergraduate mood persists, intercollegiate athletics
are going to be a target of criticism, disruption and protest.

And if you'll stop to think about it for a moment, I think
you'll agree that we are a prime target.

We're a prime target because there's a "credibility gap" between what we *profess* for intercollegiate athletics and what we
actually deliver. We have advertised some pretty grand values
for organized athletics, and have attributed to competitive sport
some virtues that should command the respect of all. But we
have, at the same time—consciously or unconsciously—trimmed
our sails to the demands of a world that is all too ready to sub-
vert those values and betray those virtues. We have compromised.
And the one thing this essentially idealistic generation finds most
offensive is compromise.

Please don't misunderstand me. Intercollegiate athletics are
quite capable of delivering as advertised. The ideals of amateur
sport are as valid today as ever. Team play and competition are
as good avenues as I know to teach a young man the thrill and
satisfaction of sublimating his personal interest to the good of
the many; for the young man who wants to ally himself with a
cause, team play is enormously gratifying and valuable. I *believe*
in the humanizing values of sport. I believe they can be what they
profess to be.

But let's be honest about it. A lot of competing and even
contradictory values have found their way into intercollegiate
competition. The felt need to gratify *spectators* has especially
taken our minds off the players. The need for revenues has, in
some cases, taken our eyes off the values of amateurism. A
craving for institutional recognition has kept us from recognizing

the participants. In a lot of ways—some of them minor, some major—we have lent credence to the notion that we pay *lip service* to the values of sport, as we so often pay lip service to peace, to improved race relations, and to academic values.

And if today's increasingly skeptical students can catch us in inconsistencies, in half-truths and in posturing, they can and will give us a lot of trouble.

Take athletic scholarships. Do you really think that an idealistic generation of students is in this day and age going to tolerate a situation in which funds are deployed to athletes at the expense of youngsters from disadvantaged communities and homes? Do you really think they'll accept the rationale that athletic scholarships help ultimately to raise money for the biology department; or that they help the old alma mater in the world of "PR"? These are, in fact, the kind of cynical, materialistic rationalizations that offend them the most.

What I'm trying to say is that we had better be prepared to answer some hard questions. Today's generation of college students isn't going to accept hackneyed justifications. They're going to ask us, "What's so great about athletics? What are the values they hold, that warrant the expenditure of institutional resources?"

And I'd like to say that these are fair questions; that they are questions we should have been asking ourselves all along; and that the insistent questioning of the younger generation—if we'll accept it for what it is—can do us all a great service.

The moral and practical question that confronts us is, "Are intercollegiate athletics to be measured in terms of what they do for the morale or budget or reputation of an institution? Or are they to be measured in terms of what they do for the participants—the standard test we have used historically in evaluating amateur athletics? Are they, in short, to be *participant oriented* or *spectator oriented?*"

Now, we will work our way out of today's dangers only if we think clearly and speak frankly. And I'm prepared to say that any war on today's dangers in intercollegiate athletics had better be a limited-objective undertaking. The fact of spectator

appeal is just that: a fact. To seek to eliminate all the dangers of
spectatorism is simply not feasible; to contain them and reduce
them is not only feasible but I think essential.

How do we go about it? What, more specifically, can a
college president or an athletic director do about it?

The fact of the matter is that the educational community—
and I include faculty and trustees along with students and
alumni—is divided on the value of intercollegiate athletics. And
even extreme views—"big-time" on the one hand and "abolition"
on the other—seem to appear in roughly equal degrees within
the educational community. Pity, then, the poor college president who tries to achieve some kind of consensus within his institution. He is destined to some degree of failure from the outset.

But I have one specific suggestion to make.

It is urgently important that we attempt to correct—to some
degree—the distortion that follows on spectator preoccupation.
We must restore to the athletic picture some of the very real
values that accrue to *participants* in competitive team sports.
The faculty member or the trustee who advocates the abolition
of football does so almost always because of his awareness of
the exploitative qualities—actual and potential—of "the spec-
tacle," which are repugnant to him. Given some understanding
of these *participant values,* this same person may at least understand why some of us want to see sports survive.

It is important that we avoid sentimental exaggeration of the
values of football—one of the historical errors of the past. Even
Delaney Kiphuth doesn't, I think, believe that playing against
Harvard is the most important thing a Yale man will ever do.
But we must get across the real values we know are there. Only
in this way can we hope to restore confidence in games that are
rapidly becoming the captive of people who know their real
thrills only vicariously, and who would distort them for purposes
ranging from ego satisfaction to crime.

We cannot justify intercollegiate athletics on any rational
basis other than their value for participants. And if spectator
values continue to obscure these—and even threaten to eliminate them—then all is lost.

But let me describe for you a course of action that one

institution—Jim Hickey's and Christy's and mine—proposes to take. A course of action that I believe will accomplish two things: demonstrate a belief in the real values of competitive team sport, and test the validity of intercollegiate athletics in this day and age.

1. We propose to provide our athletes with the finest facilities and equipment we can afford.
2. We propose to give them the best coaching that is available. And by this I mean coaches who believe in the values of the game for participants and whose first concern is for the young men entrusted to their care.
3. We propose to attract athletes to the institution solely on the basis of what the institution can do for their educational and personal development.
4. We propose to give athletes financial assistance within reasonable standards of financial need and academic performance.
5. We propose to set standards of academic and personal conduct that will represent a true challenge to participants.
6. We propose to ask our athletes to play only against teams that represent institutions of similar purpose and values.
7. We propose to broaden and enrich the intramural and recreational dimensions of our program.
8. We propose to do these things regardless of their impact on alumni giving, gate receipts, press coverage or institutional status.

There will be those who will say that even then, we will be placing too much emphasis on—paying too much attention to —intercollegiate sports. To them I can do no more than recite an old adage: "Let us not, in seeking the perfect, destroy the good."

And if, having instituted these policies, and competing under these conditions, we cannot win a respectable fraction of our intercollegiate contests over the years; if we cannot win a fair share of student and alumni and faculty and public support on the strength of these policies; then I say to you that intercollegiate athletics are beyond moral salvation. If our responsible compromise with the realities of spectatorism fails, then the in-escapable—and for me, bitter—conclusion is that we have, for all intents and purposes, destroyed something that has had and can have great value for young men. And the exploiters, inci-dentally, will have killed the goose that laid their golden egg.

I urge you to make common cause with all responsible edu-cators and athletic leaders, to restore to intercollegiate athletics that degree of integrity that has earned them your devotion and respect and affection, and, I assure you, mine.

4

The College Coach

The following article—in a somewhat abbreviated form—first appeared in Track and Field News *during the spring of 1968 under the title, "College Track Uptight." The revolt of high school and college athletes was still only simmering at the time, and I feared that the article might encounter an unresponsive audience and simply be ignored. I quickly discovered that my fear was unfounded. Much to my surprise, as well as that of the magazine's editors, the article generated a response unprecedented in the twenty-year history of the magazine. I was more than pleased with the outcome since my intention in writing the article was not to offer pat solutions but to provoke a discussion of the role of the college track coach among athletes, coaches, and fans.*

From all the responses that were published in Track and Field News *following the publication of this piece, I have chosen excerpts from eight of them—four critical, four supportive—to be reprinted in the last section of this chapter. It is not accidental that the four critical responses came from coaches while the four in support were written by athletes. The reasons for much of the conflict in athletics today become apparent when one compares the responses of the coaches with those of the athletes. One prominent West Coast track coach was so incensed by the article that he attempted to have Dick Drake, the Managing Editor of* Track and Field News *and the person who was responsible for publishing the article, fired. Although the article specifically deals with only one sport—track and field—I believe it, as well as the responses to it, are relevant in varying degrees to all interscholastic and intercollegiate sports.*

> I realised then how delicately one's individual freedom is poised. Though most of us were perhaps unaware of it, the school was in fact governed more by fear in one way or another, than by respect or tolerance. . . . Under these conditions, freedom to explore and expand was always in danger.
>
> ROGER BANNISTER (1963)

The American university track coach is a rare phenomenon. He gets a regular salary, enjoys all the fringe benefits of a faculty member, and has a large number of athletes who are required to train under his tutelage. Most coaches throughout the world are honorary—do not get paid—or operate free-lance like Percy Cerutty in Australia and Mihaly Igloi in the United States.

Athletes training under free-lance or honorary coaches have voluntarily come to the coach; the coach, therefore, is free to use whatever approach to athletics he chooses. Igloi's Napoleonic like coaching in which he dominates and directs every move his athletes make often attracts those athletes who are incapable or unwilling to think for themselves—at least with regard to their athletic activity.[1] Whereas coaches such as Mal Andrews of Cal State at Hayward or Brian Mitchell of Great Britain usually attract more self-reliant athletes.[2]

---

1. Although he is a charming man personally and a most courageous individual, Igloi's coaching methods have become increasingly authoritarian and dictatorial during the past few years (1964–68). It is especially saddening to see Igloi adopt this posture, for he himself is an independent, self-reliant person who would never tolerate the very behavior he expects his athletes to endure.

2. For those who would question my claim that an athlete's personality is reflected in his choice of a coach, I offer the following comparison. In an interview with *World Athletics* (Sept. 1962, p. 23) Jim Beatty, perhaps Igloi's most famous pupil, had this response when questioned about his hobbies, "Eating apple pie and ice cream and then going to sleep." In an interview with the same magazine (November 1961, p. 15) Adrian Metcalfe, a self-coached international level quarter-miler, was also questioned about his hobbies. Metcalfe, replying with typical British understatement, had this to say; "Rather passive I'm afraid—a keen

The non-university coach is free to make athletics an end in itself if he so desires since he is not associated with an academic institution. However, university athletics must be conducted in an educational manner; this is the only proper justification for the school sponsoring athletics.

American university students who want to compete for their schools are, with a few exceptions, required to train under the direct supervision of the coach. That the coach's personality may make him totally unfit to be working within a university—coaches are usually hired solely because of their reputations as athletes or because of their success with one or two phenomenal athletes—is seldom considered. No matter what their level of performance, students are regularly denied the opportunity to compete for their school if they want to use their own training methods, work under someone other than the "'official" coach, or train at some other time than those sacred hours, 3 P.M. to 6 P.M.

The average university coach denies he has captive athletes by saying students are free to transfer to another school or compete for a track club if they do not like him or his methods. He neglects to recognize the absurdness of making a choice of schools because of the presence of an athletic coach instead of for what educational opportunities a school may offer. Also, since

interest in the arts and in serious conversation. I also enjoy myself doodling on the piano."

This is, of course, not scientific proof of my contention, but it is an honest presentation of data. Contemporary data-collecting social scientists offer much more data in their studies, but they sometimes offer much less honesty.

Further evidence along this line is the failure of Igloi's four famous protégés—Beatty, Iharos, Tabori, and Rozavolgyi—ever to win an international title of major significance despite their having set innumerable world records—most being set in rather obscure meets. It is possible that those athletes who willingly train under Igloi's dictatorial coaching may not have the necessary self-reliance to perform up to their maximum potential in international competition where Igloi is unable to direct their every move.

Keen track observers will remember that Bob Schul won his Olympic Gold Medal after leaving Igloi. Although he incorporated many of Igloi's techniques into his training, Schul was self-coached at the Tokyo Olympics.

there are no track clubs in most areas of the country, athletes do not really have the alternative of competing for a club. And on the West Coast where there are track clubs for which university athletes could compete, coaches have repeatedly threatened reprisals against any club that would allow college athletes to compete for them.

It should be clear that these coaches, because of their association with the university, have different responsibilities and obligations than free-lance and honorary coaches. The primary responsibility of university coaches is to be educators, not developers of Olympic medal winners. If they want to put sole emphasis on developing national champions, they should leave the university and the security of a regular salary. Both Igloi and Cerutty have paid a dear price for their freedom—they have had to live in constant fear of financial impoverishment. But our university coaches want both their secure salaries and free-lance freedom.

A university coach should accommodate every student who wants to try out for the team. Of course, if the student does not perform at a high enough level, the coach has the right to say he cannot be on the team. But the coach has no right to require him to train by any particular method, just as a professor cannot force a student to study in any particular manner. Whether it be in the classroom or in the athletic arena, unless the student specifically seeks help, the professor or coach should render judgment only on the level of performance, not on the method of preparation for that performance. A student who gets an "A" on an examination deserves that grade regardless of what his study habits are, and an athlete who is the best runner on the team should be able to compete for his school regardless of how he trains.

Herb Elliott, the great Australian miler and 1960 Olympic champion, has written, " . . . the more I speak to athletes, the more convinced I become that the method of training is relatively unimportant. There are many ways to the top, and the training method you choose is just the one that suits you best" (1964, p. 103). The finest scientific investigators, after examining various training methods, have reached essentially the same conclusion as Elliott.

Most university coaches are either unfamiliar, or disagree, with Elliott's statement, for they seem to believe they have *the method*. How else could they justify dismissing from the team those students who do not follow their every dictate. If coaches believe they have the only correct method, they are wrong scientifically. And if they know they do not have the only correct method, but still force students to train under their direction, they are being sadistic and are morally wrong.

A few coaches are willing to acknowledge that there is no one correct training method, but they arrogantly conclude from this that they are therefore justified in imposing whatever method they happen to have adopted. This peculiar reasoning poignantly illustrates the authoritarian nature of the typical coach: "As long as there ain't no one best method, I'll impose any damn system I want, and if you don't like it boy, you had better get out." You are branded a "troublemaker" if you suggest that maybe athletes should be allowed to choose whatever training system they find most enjoyable and meaningful.

It is shameful, but true, that the least intelligent and least educated people in the university wield the most power. As Ernest Becker, Paul Goodman, and numerous other contemporary educators have shown, administrators, school boards and regents—and I would add athletic directors and coaches—run the show, while professors and students are essentially powerless. It may be a political reality that the least knowledgeable wield the power, but this certainly should not be the case within the university.

If a radical professor dismissed students from his sociology class because they had short hair, the administration would rebuke him immediately. However, administrators tolerate athletic coaches suspending students from university athletic teams for having long hair. The Deans of Men at most universities feel they do not have the right to regulate students' personal appearance, dating behavior, or off-campus drinking habits. Yet, university coaches dismiss athletes from the team because of "poor" personal appearance, "improper" dating behavior such as interracial dating, or even for the drinking of a few beers. And then noted sport psychologists Ogilvie and Tutko come along and label those few athletes who have the courage to resist this tyrannical control as uncoachables.[3]

Part of the traditional code of academic freedom for teachers says that since they have a captive audience in their pupils, they have no right to force their personal beliefs on these pupils. Similarly, a university coach has "captive athletes" since all students who desire to compete on the school team must train under the coach. Thus, a coach, just like a teacher, has no right to force athletes to conform to his personal beliefs about long hair, interracial dating, or any other personal matters.

Only those individuals who are doing nothing meaningful with their lives will have the time, or disposition, to be obsessed with insignificant trivia such as the length of someone's hair. It makes me more sad than angry to think that grown men—men who like to call themselves educators—have nothing more important to do than inspect the shoes of their athletes to see if they are properly shined. If these coaches own a shoe polish company or have an interest in the barber industry, they might better be honest and admit it instead of preaching that the worth of a human being is determined by the length of his hair or the degree of shine on his shoes!

A student who is attempting to be a serious scholar while

3. Rollo May, a humanistic existential psychologist, has this to say about rebels such as the many fine university students who are rebelling against paternalistic authoritarianism, " 'Give me liberty or give me death' is not necessarily histrionic or evidence of a neurotic attitude. Indeed, there is reason for believing that it may represent the most mature form of distinctively human behavior" (1967, p. 36). In many instances, those individuals that Ogilvie and Tutko are helping to label uncoachable and our university coaches are branding as troublemakers may very well be the most mentally healthy athletes.

In the athletic world, sagacious Percy Cerutty recognizes that these authoritarian coaches are driving our finest youth right out of athletics. "What these 'authoritative' coaches, these 'do-this-and that' teachers, these schedule addicts, are responsible for in destroying the natural joys and responses in the young athlete can never be truly known. But it must result in the loss of thousands annually in any country of reasonable size and population" (1962, p. 14).

at the same time trying to participate in athletics will find it to his advantage to be schizophrenic. A good university student is inquisitive, argumentative, and one who accepts nothing without a thorough investigation. But sport psychologists Ogilvie and Tutko, in their book *Problem Athletes and How to Handle Them,* a book widely praised by American coaches, say athletes are resisting coaching when: "There is a tendency to be argumentative . . . ; The athlete will use other authorities in an attempt to refute the coaches arguments . . . ; They try to catch the coach making inconsistent statements and to find flaws in his arguments" (1966, p. 33).

Apparently our university students are supposed to question the most intelligent members of the academic community, the professors; but they risk the stigma of being branded uncoachable if they rigorously question their coach. If a coach wants to call himself an educator, it is only reasonable that he should expect to be treated as one.

Ogilvie and Tutko, like most other contemporary social scientists who believe their work can exist in a value-free vacuum, never took the time to examine the structure of intercollegiate athletics before writing their book. A few of the many unwritten assumptions behind their book are that coaches are moral men, men who have the interests of their athletes at heart, and men who know more about athletic techniques than their athletes know. If these assumptions can be questioned, and I certainly believe that in many cases they can,[4] their book does a grave disservice to college athletes throughout America. Unless they are willing to examine the proper role of university athletics, Ogilvie and Tutko would do well to restrict their "sport psychologizing" to the realm of professional athletics where their work as industrial psychologists might be relevant. Attempts to apply their work to university athletics are as misdirected as California Governor Ronald Reagan's attempts to subject his state's system of higher education to a cost-benefit analysis study. Ogilvie and Tutko, along with Reagan, do not seem to understand that the

4. Even such widely respected magazines as *Newsweek* (July 15, 1968) and *Sports Illustrated* (July 1, 8, 15, 22, 29; 1968) have acknowledged the deplorable behavior of many American university coaches.

purposes and goals of a university are not necessarily the same as those of a large corporation.

The only clear-cut responsibility of the university coach is to select the best athletes for the team, and this can be accomplished by trials in the same manner we select our Olympic team. Additionally, the coach can handle administrative matters such as arranging the meet schedule. He has innumerable opportunities to demonstrate his competence (both as a teacher of athletic techniques and educator), and athletes will willingly seek the coach's assistance if they feel he has something to offer.[5]

Most certainly, the coach has no right to interfere with a student's personal and social life. The best athletes should be selected for the team as long as they are in good standing with the general university rules—rules that apply equally to all students. A university can have a track team without a coach, but as many college coaches are beginning to discover, it is difficult to have a team without athletes. A coach is—or should be—hired to serve those students who choose to participate in athletics, not to berate them. He is the most expendable part of university athletics and he should be summarily dismissed if he is not doing his job.[6]

5. It is undoubtedly true that most athletes will willingly subject themselves to the whimsy of anyone who calls himself a coach. As Cerutty writes, it is not easy to be a responsible, self-reliant person. "I have said it, and I repeat it, the hardest, and most painful thing that anyone can do is—to *think:* to be independent of others; self-reliant, a leader and a champion. It is equally true that the many do not want to be self-reliant, to be leaders. They are content to follow, to adopt anyone's schedules, to let anyone think for them, decide for them . . ." (1964, p. 122).

Brian Mitchell, a perceptive British Honorary Senior Coach, concurs with Cerutty. In one of the few quality articles in Fred Wilt's garrulous book, *Run, Run, Run,* Mitchell says, ". . . it is rare to come across an athlete who will not settle for mere instruction but seeks to find out for himself, and seeks help only from somebody else when he is convinced that another person wishes to understand as deeply as he himself does" (1965, p. 247). Despite this lack of courage on the part of most athletes, there still are some rare spirits who want to seek their own authentic way, and our university system of athletics should not punish these athletes—if anything, they should be rewarded.

6. Berny Wagner, track coach at Oregon State, openly admits that coaches are not hired to serve university athletes, but to please "alumni

Our best educators do not have to require students to attend their lectures. Only those professors who feel they have nothing to offer require class attendance, for they know few students would come if attendance were voluntary. If university athletic coaches have something to offer their athletes, they will not have to require students to train under them. Could it be that these coaches realize that, in fact, they have nothing to offer?

THE RESPONSE

JIM BUSH, *head track coach at UCLA:* This article comparing college coaches with coaches that are not associated with colleges is one of the most ridiculous statements I have ever heard. Evidently Scott knows very little about some of the top notch track coaches in the world. I know Mihaly Igloi, Arthur Lydiard, plus others, and you either train according to their plans or you do not train with them. I cannot see any difference in making an athlete train the way you want him to if he is on your college team.

I believe Scott answers all his statements when he quotes Herb Elliott ". . . the more I speak to athletes, the more convinced I become that the method of training is relatively unimportant. There are many ways to the top, and the training method you choose is just the one that suits you best." Then he goes on to say ". . . the finest scientific investigators, after examining various training methods, have reached essentially the same conclusions as Elliott." So if each coach thinks he has a "method," who is the athlete to say the coach is wrong and the athlete right?

The majority of the athletes get a lot more out of it than they ever put into it! And how many athletes who have broken away

---

and other interested private parties" (1968, p. 8) who finance university athletic programs. Sensitive, honest coaches such as Forrest Jamieson, "Hap" Hardell, Tracey Walters, and Pete Petersons have recognized this and, consequently, they have refused to work within the American intercollegiate athletic system. The failure of university athletics is obvious when these four outstanding coaches find the system so repulsive that they are forced to refuse to cooperate with it despite their enormous love for athletics.

from college coaches have gone on to be successful on their own training methods? Almost always these complaining drop-outs are either underachievers or out-and-out failures who use the coach as an excuse for their own lack of success.

I really resent the statement that the least intelligent and least educated people in the university wield the most power—the person who believes this is true is sick and badly in need of help. Some of his other statements are so idiotic I do not want even to answer them.

BRUCE KIDD, *Canadian distance runner and graduate student at the University of Chicago:* Jack Scott's description about the authoritarian nature of US college sport (Opinion 68, II March *T&FN*) would generally square with my impressions of it. (There are exceptions: Ted Haydon here at Chicago has about the most mature approach to coaching of any man I've ever met.) I wonder, however, if the restrictiveness which Scott criticizes is solely characteristic of campus sport, or is rather a part of American higher education as a whole. Certainly in other countries and continents where the college athlete assumes comparatively much more responsibility for his activity, university life in general offers more individual freedom too.

One of the reasons I never accepted a scholarship in the US seven years ago was the unnecessarily onerous dual meet schedules of most colleges. I remember telling one coach of my ambitions to be a six-miler, and he responded he thought that with my strength I might even be able to run a leg on the mile relay team in dual meets after I had run the 880, mile and two-mile.

It's always extremely difficult to pinpoint causes for complex attitudes such as those toward sports in American colleges, especially when attitudes toward sport are so closely bound up with the other dominant values in a culture. But it's my own feeling that until college track ceases to be a crusade and once again becomes a sport, it will continue to be "uptight."

PETE MORGAN, *Princeton track coach:* I am only a coach and suffer from the cerebral spasms referred to by the budding psychologists. If I were to summarize Jack Scott's treatise, it would be simply "let's do away with discipline in all forms." We could then get to know ourselves and truly appreciate culture, art and love in their refined realms. It may be of interest to the learned doctor that since the early 30s progressive education has been doing just that. What do we have today? A country breaking apart at the seams; the lack of respect for authority and laws may just help Dr. Scott to eliminate coaching as a profession. This won't be the only casualty; all the cherished principles and desires of its citizens will evaporate. Freedom of everything is the theme of today's rationalizers. I am not ready to join Dr. Scott's evangelical movement at this time. Possibly you might add my name to his list defending motherhood and the flag. My apologies for this hour of unventing pent-up emotions.

HUGH SWEENY, *Princeton track athlete:* Nowhere in Jack Scott's article does he say that every athlete knows instinctively how to train. He says the athlete "should seek the coach's assistance if he feels the coach has something to offer." Most athletes are in that category. They don't read "Track Technique" and they would profit from the advice of a knowledgable coach. But my observations are that athletes who want to use their own methods are track enthusiasts, with knowledge of the current "state of the art." They train individually to get better results; at the same time they are often working harder than those on the team using the coach's method. For example, Bob Deines and Amby Burfoot perform up to any coach's standards on the track but could never have approached their performances at Boston using standard track training. How can Scott's critics say these men lack discipline. Self-discipline, a far more valuable trait than authoritarian discipline, is what the athlete has who knows his goal and cuts his own path to success. Perhaps one reason why so many American athletes retire after college graduation is that the idea of team performance is so deeply engrained in their mentality that they have no goals of their own to strive for later.

BOB GIEGENGACK, *Yale University track coach and head U.S. Olympic coach in 1964:* Just who or what is Jack Scott? What are his qualifications that any of us should engage him in dialogue? From what Olympian heights of academic or athletic achievement does he pontificate? Unsupported generalizations by Scott or Bannister serve no purpose except to set up convenient straw-men who succumb to ill placed and awkward attack.

Where do "administrators and coaches wield the most power while professors and students are essentially powerless?"!!! A preposterous statement made up out of whole cloth without an iota of truth. Who is to say who are the least-educated and least-intelligent in the university? Jack Scott? All American coaches are university trained and often in more than one discipline. Shall we submit to IQ tests? Will Scott take the same along with his honorary coaches?

Coaches either contribute to the educational level or should get out, and with their "average" education and intelligence easily earn greater material rewards. Our confidence in the value of our ideals and our discipline so lacking in most areas repay us for our personal sacrifice and dedication.

Parents, administrators and even educators have in too many cases abdicated their responsibilities. An undisciplined man is an uneducated one no matter the number of letters after his name. In a world gone permissive, a touch of paternalism is all to the good. Our pupils are grateful and support the rules of training even if Scott doesn't. If the Sociology prof tolerates lack of common courtesy, disrespect, boorish manners and sloppy and unclean dress, he does so because he doesn't have the "guts" to demand respect or possibly does not deserve it, not because the administrators will fire him if he expects good manners.

None should accept such a ridiculous caricature of the American university track and field coach.

JOHN DOBROTH, *7-foot high jumper and law student at UCLA:* I'd like to add a point or two to the fine article by Jack Scott. It was something that needed to be said. The recent comments by UCLA coach Jim Bush after the defeat by Kansas, when he said, "I've never had a team fold up on me like this one did today; it was the worst performance of any team I've coached in six years," and called the loss a "disgraceful performance," show the extent of this system's corruption. Can you imagine the university professor blaming his students for not making him look good? Professors and coaches are paid to teach, not insult. Yet, a track coach can publicly condemn his entire team for failure to meet his standards. The implication of blaming the team for letting him down is that when they do win, they do it for him. Further, it implies that university men won't honor a commitment made to a team to do their best. Are college athletes considered professionals whose lives on and off the field are the property of an employer?

The basic point of Scott's paper is that these coaches are so sure winning is important—and that they know how to go about winning—that any means used to improve performance is justified. Thus, they manipulate the man without regard for what is really healthy for the individual make-up of that person. They may not, and I've seen it, talk to that athlete for days at a time. They must request that a boy compete or train while injured. They may reflect on his masculinity. All to get him to perform at a higher level. I don't accuse these men of overt cruelty. They simply do not see that improving at track is not worth the athlete's psychological or physical well being. If a "soft" or insecure boy is intimidated by a strong-willed (sun-tanned, button-down) coach, he will feel guilt for not coming up to this strong figure's conception of an athlete and man. If the boy is perceptive he recognizes the absurdity of a system in which a man who is there to offer help and resources acts as an omniscient being.

I read Mr. Scott's article to over 100 coaches at some recent clinics in Los Angeles. Several in the audience expressed to me that authoritarian coaching was good, since students (at some indefinite age) cannot know right from wrong, cannot think for themselves and cannot make good judgments on their own—and therefore need control. My question is, in what part of a young man's life is he free to fail? Not social areas. Not scholastic. Not athletic. If you are insulated from failure, you can't take credit for success. Are we sure we know the way for people to live, compete and dress? If we are, let's not pretend we believe in freedom or dissent.

BERNY WAGNER, *head track coach at Oregon State University:*
To my knowledge, Scott has not been a successful college athlete
either working with a coach or without one; so his qualifications
to criticize might be questioned.

I believe that if success were necessary for the academic professor, he too would control and direct the study habits and social behavior affecting success or detracting from it. I believe,
too, that students would find success more often than they do.

Athletics at most universities are largely paid for and supported by donations from alumni and other interested private
parties. The coach must be aware of where the money is coming from and must have a responsibility to the people who are
financing the facilities, equipment, travel, athletic financial aid to
students, etc. The privilege of having these things does not come
free. The alums of another era have their own ideas about what
an athlete should look like and how he should behave even if
they themselves possibly did not behave this way. It is difficult,
perhaps, for a man who competed some years ago when athletes
wore short hair to make a substantial donation to a program in
which athletes wear beards and long hair. Perhaps the time will
come when alums of another era will find it difficult to support
athletes with skinned heads or crew cuts.

It is easy to be a critic, but difficult to endure the many
problems, sacrifices and hard work necessary for success. Jack
Scott has evidently decided on the former course.

DR. SIDNEY GENDIN, *former college distance runner, presently
assistant professor in philosophy, State University of New York
at Stony Brook:* The ill-conceived comments by Mssrs. Wagner,
Giegengack and Bush on Jack Scott's article cannot go unan-
swered. I shall limit my remarks to Mr. Wagner's letter since his
is the most detailed reply of the three.

1) He makes the absurd remark that since Scott was not a
successful athlete his qualifications to criticize are questionable;
Scott was not presenting himself as an expert. Rather he was
criticizing the rights of coaches to interfere with the personal free-
doms of their athletes. Whether the coach knows more about
training is not the point. Those athletes who wish to take advan-

tage of the coach's knowledge are free to do so. The others should not be penalized for not doing so. Questioning Scott's right to criticize—not merely the correctness of his criticisms—is an example of the authoritarianism Scott deplores.

2) Wagner maintains that if college professors were publicly evaluated several times each year, they, too, would try to control the social behavior of their students. This nonsensical speculation is the best he can do to justify his own disciplinarianism. Speaking as one of those about whom Wagner speculates, I can say that Scott's point was that if professors tried to control students' lives as rigidly as coaches do, the attempts would not be tolerated for long.

3) He makes much of the fact that university athletics is big business. Since the university is sinking so much money into financing the student-athlete he better cooperate or else! So far as I can see this is only an argument against big business athletics. Wagner says that rightly or wrongly crew-cut alumni of yesteryear won't donate money to a program in which athletes wear long hair. Well, the short answer to this is that it is the "wrongly" which applies. Why should students be blackmailed by the stupid prejudices of middle-aged alumni?

5

Football and Education

BY DAVE MEGGYESY

Many concerned educators have been struggling since the 1890s to eliminate the abuses of big-time college athletics. By 1905 the abuses in intercollegiate athletics, especially football, had become so widespread that a group of educators led by Chancellor McCracken of New York University formed the Intercollegiate Athletic Association of the United States, an organization that was supposed to reform college athletics. The National Collegiate Athletic Association (NCAA) was founded in 1910 as an outgrowth of this group. At that time, the NCAA announced its objective as being "the regulation and supervision of college athletics throughout the United States in order that the athletic activities of the colleges and universities of the United States may be maintained on an ethical plane in keeping with the dignity and high purpose of education" (Scott, 1951, p. 33).

A thoroughly documented report on college athletics published in 1929 by the Carnegie Foundation revealed that the abuses so common at the turn of the century had been in no way attenuated and, in many cases, were even more rampant. Quite clearly, the NCAA, in its first nineteen years of existence, did not meet its stated objective of maintaining intercollegiate athletics "on an ethical plane in keeping with the dignity and high purpose of education." Contemporary reports of journalists and educators have shown that the NCAA is still no closer to meeting its original objective than it was in 1929. In fact, quite ironically, today the NCAA is the organization most responsible for the big-time, commercialized nature of college athletics. The NCAA is now the main force perpetuating the very conditions it was created to eliminate!

The Institute for the Study of Sport and Society was founded in the spring of 1970 with one of its chief purposes being to examine the role of athletics in American higher education. The failure of documents such as the 1929 Carnegie Foundation report to bring about any meaningful changes in intercollegiate athletics indicated to those of us at the Institute that a purely academic approach to the problem was obviously not sufficient. One of our assumptions was that these scholarly reports, in their attempt to objectively state the facts, did not adequately portray the effect participation in big-time intercollegiate athletics has on the individual participants. We felt that personal statements from sensitive, intelligent individuals who had participated in big-time college athletics might create an impetus for change that the dry, factual, scholarly reports had been unable to generate. It was with this purpose in mind that we came upon the idea of autobiographical documentaries—books and articles that, while portraying an athlete's personal story, would also document the state of organized athletics in our society. We felt that certain select athletes, aided by the facilities and expertise of those associated with the Institute, would be able to produce autobiographical works that would go far beyond the scope of the traditional sport book.

The first such book to be written at the Institute was Dave Meggyesy's Out of Their League. *The quality of this book and the reaction to it by the sports establishment indicate that these autobiographical documentaries will not be summarily dismissed as were the earlier academic reports. Though Meggyesy's book covers his entire football career, including his seven years as a linebacker with the St. Louis Cardinals, the following excepts were taken from the chapters that examined his college football years.*

Shortly after I graduated from high school I went down to visit two cousins in Baton Rouge, Louisiana. One of them had played defensive end for the Chinese Bandits, on the Louisiana

Dave Meggyesy, former college All-American and seven years pro football linebacker for the St. Louis Cardinals, working on his book, *Out of Their League,* at the Institute for the Study of Sport and Society. Dave and I worked together at the Institute for six months writing his book. Assisting athletes such as Meggyesy in the writing of articles and books about their athletic experiences is one of the many projects the Institute sponsors (*Photo courtesy Micki Scott*).

State University national champion team of 1958. His younger brother, Gary, who was entering LSU in the fall, was a high school All-American. My cousins' house was near the LSU campus and we spent a lot of time during my visit hanging around with some of the big-name LSU jocks like Billy Cannon and Warren Rabb. Gary and I worked out every day with many of the LSU football players, doing a lot of calisthenics and running. One morning we were working out by Tiger Stadium when Head Coach Paul Dietzel and a few of his assistants wandered by. They asked some of the players who I was and that afternoon they called Gary's home and offered me a scholarship. Though I was still planning on going to Syracuse on the football scholarship they had offered me, I was very interested in LSU. They were the National Champions and Baton Rouge was the most football crazy town I had ever seen. The people were falling all over their feet to be with or to know football players. I told Dietzel I'd accept his offer, and he told me my parents' signature on a letter of intent would be needed before I could be officialy awarded a scholarship. He tried hard to get me to handle the whole thing by mail, and Gary's parents also wanted me to stay in Baton Rouge, but my parents insisted I come home and talk the whole matter over with them.

By the time I got home I was really in a turmoil. I called Coach Bell at Syracuse to tell him I had decided to go to LSU. He asked me how I could do such a thing to him after he had personally recruited me. Within five minutes after I stopped talking with Bell, Ben Schwartzwalder, the head football coach at Syracuse, called. As usual, he did not waste any words. "Boy, you fly up here immediately. We'll pay for the plane," he told me, "Just get up here by tomorrow." No sooner had Schwartzwalder hung up than I received a call from Col. Byrne, head of the Air Force ROTC program at Syracuse. The Colonel said he had just talked with Ben Schwartzwalder and was calling because he had learned I was interested in becoming a jet pilot. He personally assured me I would be able to go through the Air Force ROTC program and could enter flight school when I graduated from college.

I arrived in Syracuse the next day and was met at the airport

by Jim Shrieve, the freshman coach. He took me to my room at
the Hotel Syracuse and then left, saying he would return with
Coach Bell at six o'clock for dinner. I waited around by myself
for about two hours feeling anxious as hell. About six Bell called
to tell me they were waiting for me in the hotel dining room. I
walked down and saw what seemed to me to be the entire Syracuse coaching staff sitting there with one empty chair reserved for
me. Schwartzwalder, the head coach, whom I had met only
briefly on my recruiting trip to Syracuse, was at the head of the
table. Seated around him were Bell, Shrieve, and Joe Szombathy,
the end coach who was there to play on my ethnic sensibilities because he too was of Hungarian descent. The chair reserved for
me was directly across from Ben and I couldn't escape his gaze.
Ben talks in this raspy, gravelly voice. His head is usually lowered and he peers at you over the top of his glasses. Bill Bell sat
there, asking every few minutes how I could do this to him. He
looked hurt. The waitress came over to take our order, but Ben
shooed her away. She must have known I was starved, for she
came back about every ten minutes. Ben never took his eyes off
me, never stopped talking. "Boy, we had great plans for you,"
Ben would say, and Szombathy or Shrieve would second him.
They really came on heavy against LSU. Shrieve told me, "Dave, if
you told us you wanted to go to Notre Dame, or some other fine
school, we wouldn't say anything. But we would be doing you an
injustice if we didn't object to your going to LSU." Even though
the public schools I had gone to in Ohio were always all white,
they made a big point of telling me "There will be no colored students at LSU." After a while they began to focus on how Syracuse was a small school with a limited number of scholarships
and how it would be impossible for them to give my scholarship
to someone else at this late date. I finally agreed to go to Syracuse. They were all smiles and assured me how happy I would
be. Then Ben finally allowed the waitress to come over and take
our orders.

The next morning Coach Bell picked me up at the hotel to
take me to the airport for my flight back to Ohio. Col. Byrne, the
Air Force ROTC commander whom I had talked to briefly on the
phone was with him in the car. When we arrived at the Syracuse

airport, Bell drove over to the National Guard hanger, and Col. Byrne got out to speak with some of the Guardsmen stationed there. He asked me if I would like to sit in a jet, so I climbed up, and he spent a few minutes explaining the controls. Once I was back in Solon, Coach Bell would call me every week to see how I was doing and to tell me how personally pleased he was that I was going to Syracuse. He assured me he would do anything he could to make my four years at Syracuse as enjoyable as possible. I would always reassure him that I was coming to Syracuse, and thank him for the personal interest he had in me.

For incoming freshman football players, practice began at Syracuse on September 5th even though classes did not start for another two weeks. I took a train from Cleveland to Syracuse and arrived tired from a night made sleepless by excitement and anticipation over the beginning of college. After collecting my luggage I immediately telephoned Coach Bell who had insisted that I call him the minute I got into town so he could pick me up at the station and get me settled in the football living quarters. His phone rang for a very long time and I was just about ready to hang up when he answered. Our conversation went something like this: "Hello Coach Bell? This is Dave. I just arrived and I'm down at the train station." There was a long silence and I started to get a little nervous. "Do you realize what the hell time it is?" he growled. "Yes, Coach, it's about 6:20 in the morning." By this time he was really pissed and told me to meet him at the Syracuse Gym around 9 o'clock. Since I didn't know my way around town, I asked him how I should go about getting there. "I don't care," he responded, "Just don't ever wake me up this early in the morning again."

We had two practice sessions a day for a week and didn't get our first break until freshman orientation day. It seemed like we had been at Syracuse for ages, and right from the start we didn't feel much fellowship with the other freshmen. When I saw them running around the quadrangle in their orange beanies it hit me how different I was. On the one hand, I felt somewhat superior, but on the other hand they made me realize I was part of a select group of individuals brought there to play football, not to have a "normal" college experience.

The following day we had to register for courses. Syracuse had a special remedial program, ostensibly designed to help freshmen entering with academic deficiencies. But the coaching staff encouraged me and the other freshmen football players to enroll in this program because it lasted through the whole year and consisted of mainly "Mickey Mouse" courses requiring little work.

Joe Szombathy, the varsity end coach, was also in charge of the athletic tutoring program. He would take the freshmen football players' class cards and simply fill out the courses he wanted them to take. Szombathy not only enrolled most of them in the remedial program, but decided on their courses with one of the main criterion being whether or not they interfered with afternoon football practice. I had searched through the course catalogue for classes I wanted to take, then filled out my own course card and presented it to Szombathy. He was furious. "What the hell do you think you're doing, Meggyesy?" he shouted at me. "We want you to take these other courses so you'll be sure to be eligible. You can always take the other courses next year." But I was conscious of not wanting to be identified as a stupid jock, and I refused to allow him to sway me. I simply wanted to take the courses other freshman were required to take.

We finished an undefeated freshman season. Meanwhile, the varsity was 7 and 0 and the number one ranked college team in the nation. It was exciting to be a part of the football program at that time for it seemed all the energies of the university were being channelled toward making sure we won the National Championship. Most of the varsity players had stopped going to classes and were devoting full time to football. Besides the regular afternoon practices, much of the day was spent in special team meetings. The athletic department had complete backing from the administration in this quest for a national championship. Les Dye, the Director of Admissions, had started at Syracuse as a football coach and made sure good players were admitted. Eric Faigle, the Dean of the School of Arts and Sciences, was an avid supporter of the football program and no professor was about to incur his wrath and rule a player ineligible simply because he wasn't attending classes or taking exams. Even though most of the players hadn't seen a classroom for some time, no one was declared ineligible and the team went on to win the National Championship and defeat Texas in the Cotton Bowl.

Syracuse recruited top football players regardless of their academic ability, and the athletic department's biggest jobs were to get the football players admitted and then to keep them eligible. I remember one citizenship course which all Syracuse freshmen, including football players in the remedial program, were required to take. I knew most of the other players hadn't been to class or done any studying and I couldn't figure out how they were going to pass the exam. Then, just before midterms, we had a squad meeting with one of the tutors hired by the athletic department. The tutor didn't exactly give us the test questions but he did give us a lot of important information. He told us cryptically that if we copied down what he said we would do all right on the exam. He wasn't joking: when I took the exam I discovered he had given us the answers to the test questions. When the general tutoring session broke up the tutor asked about ten ball players to stay. These were the guys who were really out of it and made no pretense about being students. They had neither the ability nor interest to do college work. I don't know exactly what kind of help they got after we left but I do know it was this kind of tutoring that kept them eligible for four years.

There were even less ethical techniques than these. For example, my brother, Dennis, who also came up to Syracuse on a football scholarship, flunked his freshman year. He was told he would have to get six units of "A" during summer school to get back in school and be eligible for football. After registering for summer school, Dennis immediately drove back to Ohio, where he spent the summer working for a Cleveland construction company. He returned to Syracuse in September with six units of "A" for courses he had never attended.

By the time I graduated, I knew it was next to impossible to be a legitimate student and a football player too. There is a clear conflict, and it is always resolved on the side of the athletic program. Nearly every major university in the country has an employee within the athletic department who supposedly provides athletes with tutorial assistance. At the University of Texas, he is known as the Brain Coach while at Berkeley he has the more prestigious title of Academic Coordinator. Whatever he is called, his task is always the same: to keep athletes eligible by whatever means necessary, even if it involves getting them an early look at exams, or hiring graduate students to write their term papers or to take finals for them.

Most athletes are accustomed to being on the take and think the system works for them or that they are somehow beating it. But the reality is quite different, and, as in most other things, the athlete is far more sinned against than sinning. He is a commodity and he is treated with unbelievable cynicism. The minute his eligibility expires, the athletic department's concern for his welfare suddenly evaporates. The free tutoring stops and an athlete finds himself faced with a flock of difficult classes which somebody has put off to keep him eligible. He finds himself encased in the stereotype of the dumb jock and psychologically devastated. Of the 26 players who got scholarships in my freshman year, only John Mackey (now an all-pro end with Baltimore), Gene Stancin and I graduated with our class.

We lost to Army in a game played in New York City, 9–6. I got a big thrill out of playing in the home of the New York Yankees, but I'll always remember that game for something else. Mark Weber had suffered a succession of knee injuries during the season, and there was some question about whether he would be able to play against Army. Mark was seriously thinking about quitting football. About a month earlier, he had asked Ben to cut him in on some of the money other players were getting. Ben flatly refused. Mark and I talked about it a lot, and he decided to stick it out because it was his last year.

He didn't even finish that year. In the second half of the Army game, Ben sent Mark in to receive a punt—something he was almost never called on to do. Mark caught it and started up field. One of Army's big tackles got a clean shot on his bad knee and just tore it up. Mark was carried off the field on a stretcher. It just didn't make sense to have a big, heavy guy with a bad knee returning a punt which everyone knows is one of the most hazardous plays in the game. Mark never played football again.

Schwartzwalder and I appeared together on a couple of radio and television shows shortly before my sophomore season ended. Since I had won honorable mention All-American honors, he was touting me as the next Roger Davis—Syracuse's great All-American lineman who also came from Solon High. I took the praise but, especially after what happened to Mark Weber, I wasn't playing football for any great love of the game but primarily to win approval. I still felt ambivalent about hitting. At times I didn't want to touch anyone or to be touched. On other occasions I felt great pleasure and release from the sheer physical violence of the game. Sometimes after getting a clean shot at the ball carrier, I would feel this tremendous energy flow and not experience the pain of contact at all. I sometimes could psych myself so high I would feel indestructible. Like most of the other players, I had been introduced to a system of rewards—psychological and material—and I played mainly for them. The intrinsic joy of physicality got shunted into the background. Even now, after playing for 14 years, I can't really say if there is any basic worth to the game. I just can't separate the game from the payoffs —approval, money, adulation.

The process of questioning, which eventually made me decide to get out of football, really began after my successful sophomore season. I had performed well and gotten recognition, but there was no real satisfaction. Shortly after the season ended, I began making friends with graduate students and people in the liberal arts. When Schwartzwalder found out about this he called me into his office. "Dave, you have a great football career ahead of you," he began. "But if you hang around with those beatniks you're going to destroy yourself." I told him they were my friends. "That may be true, Dave, but it doesn't look good for our football team for you to be hanging out with those beatniks." I assured him I would do nothing to hurt the team and left his office.

My beatnik friends, as Ben called them, hung out at a bar

near campus called the Orange. Their view of the world and of life was completely different from the football ethic. At first I couldn't believe them. They were completely sacrilegious when it came to athletics. They would get drunk and go to the games to laugh at fans and mock the coach.

Some of them were drama students and they would do great imitations of Ben, who they called "the pygmy paratrooper" because of his diminutive size and widely publicized war exploits. They would point out the cynicism and hypocrisy of the university's commitment to football: at the same time Chancellor Tolley was claiming to be guided by the highest religious and educational principles, he was hiring football players to gather prestige and money for the university. What my new friends were saying didn't make too much sense to me yet, but I enjoyed rapping with them. My association with these "beatniks" eventually became such a contradiction that I had to stop seeing them whenever I was playing. In the fall and during spring practice I would rarely stop in at the Orange for I knew hanging around there would screw me up for football.

One of the justifications for college football is that it is not only a character-builder, but a body-builder as well. This is nonsense. Young men are having their bodies destroyed, not developed. As a matter of fact, few players can escape from college football without some form of permanent disability. During my four years I accumulated a broken wrist, separations of both shoulders, an ankle that was torn up so badly it broke the arch of my foot, three major brain concussions, and an arm that almost had to be amputated because of improper treatment. And I was one of the lucky ones.

When a player is injured, he is sent to the team physician who is usually more concerned with getting the athlete back into action than anything else. This reversal of priorities leads to unbelievable abuses. One of the most common is to "shoot" a player before a game to numb a painful injured area that would normally keep him out of action. He can play, but in so doing he can also get new injuries in that part of his body where he has no feeling.

When I spoke to a group of athletes at the University of California in the Spring of 1970, Jim Calkins, co-captain of the Cal football team, told me that the coaching staff and the team physician had put him on anabolic steroids. Both assured him such drugs would make him bigger and stronger, and this is true. But they didn't bother to tell him that there are potentially dangerous side-effects. "I gained a lot of weight like they told me I would, but after a month or so, these steroids really began to fuck me up" Jim told me. "I went to the team physician and he admitted that there are possible bad side-effects. I had complete faith in the coaches and medical staff before this, and I felt betrayed." And well he might, because steroids are known to have caused atrophied testes, blunting of sex drives, damage to liver and glands, and some physicians believe they are the causal agent for cancer of the prostate. And they are widely used.

The violent and brutal player that television viewers marvel over on Saturdays and Sundays is often a synthetic product. When I got to the National Football League, I saw players taking not only steroids, but also amphetamines and barbiturates at an astonishing rate. Most NFL trainers do more dealing in these drugs than the average junky. I was glad when Houston Ridge, the San Diego Chargers' veteran defensive tackle, filed a huge suit last spring against his club, charging them with conspiracy and malpractice in the use of drugs. He charged that steroids, amphetamines, barbiturates and the like were used "not for purpose of treatment and cure, but for the purpose of stimulating mind and body so he (the player) would perform more violently as a professional. . . ."

I don't mean that players are given drugs against their will. Like Calkins, most players have complete trust in their coaches and team doctors and in the pattern of authority they represent. Associated with this is the atmosphere of suspicion which surrounds any injured player unless his injury is a visible one, like a broken bone. Coaches constantly question the validity of a player's complaints, and give him the silent treatment when he has a "suspicious" injury. The coaches don't say, "We think you're faking, don't you want to play football?" They simply stop talking to a player and the message comes across very clearly. Most players

want and need coaches' approval, especially when they are injured and can't perform, and it really tears them up when the
coach won't even speak to them. This is especially true in college
where the players are young and usually identify closely with the
coach. After a few days of this treatment, many players become
frantic. They will plead with the team physician to shoot them
up so they can play. The player will totally disregard the risk of
permanent injury.

Though we were supposed to be a superior team and were
heavily favored, we just barely managed to beat Boston College.
We celebrated after the game, not so much because we had won,
but because the weight and pressure of a particularly rough season was behind us and we were looking forward to a return to
normal life. No such luck: a few days later the Syracuse athletic
department and the college administration announced that the
team had accepted an invitation to play in the Liberty Bowl. Even
then, straight as I was, my first reaction was that the coaches and
administrators should play the game since they had accepted the
invitation. This game, which was played in Philadelphia in the
middle of December, was at best second-rate, and all it meant to
most of the players was another couple of weeks of practice. But
it was quite a profitable venture for the athletic department. The
game was nationally televised, and even though both the teams
—Syracuse and Miami—were mediocre they were invited because each had one of the country's most exciting players—our
Ernie Davis and Miami's quarterback George Mira, one of the
top passers in the history of college football. The Syracuse athletic department would get a significant amount of the television
money and they weren't about to pass this up simply because the
players were tired.

Many of us felt that since we had to play we should at least
get something out of it. After speaking to Ben, Dick Easterly, one
of the co-captains, informed us there were no plans to give the
players anything. This made us even more angry, because we
knew that players in the major bowls always received a wrist-
watch, a set of luggage or something like that. We were in a
murderously petty mood, and had a special team meeting with-

out the coaches to discuss what we should do. Some of the seniors favored boycotting the game unless the athletic department at least gave us a watch, and we decided to send the co-captains to Lou Andreas, the athletic director, to tell him this.

The athletic department had never seen the ball players get together on their own before and this, coupled with the talk of boycott, made them quickly agree to give us watches—and before the game as we had demanded. That was a good lesson: one of the greatest absurdities in the football mythology is that the players' interest are identical with those of coaches and administrators.

After the season I began to think a lot about what the football program at Syracuse meant. The whole Liberty Bowl experience had made me realize the blatantly commercial nature of college football and see that the players had picked up these petty, small-minded values. But it was also clear that I was basically just a hired hand brought in from Ohio, and that if I began to question the values behind the game very loudly, I'd quickly find myself back in Solon. We were semi-professionals, and the only reason the N.C.A.A. regulated scholarship money was to keep our wages down. We were a cheap labor pool that made great profits for the university while we were constantly told to be grateful for the opportunity we were getting. Still, standing out there like the pot of gold at the end of the rainbow, was the incentive of pro ball which helped keep the players from griping too loud or really organizing.

You hear a lot about how football scholarships allow poor kids to attend college. This may be true, but it isn't anything to be proud of. It's pretty obvious that this country could, if it wished, give everyone a chance to go to college. Actually, people should feel guilty rather than chauvinistic and elated when they see a scholarship awarded to a student who can throw a football 60 yards while one of his classmates with good grades who sincerely wants to attend college cannot do so for financial reasons.

It's not surprising that vast numbers of poor kids, black and white, throughout the country spend an inordinate amount of time and energy on athletics. Thousands upon thousands of them turn out for high school football every year, filled with dreams of gridiron glory and hopes of a college scholarship and immortality as a pro. Instead of talking honestly, most high school coaches play cynically upon these dreams and hopes. Figures released in 1969 by the N.C.A.A. present a sobering reality: only one out of every 30 high school football players ever gets a chance to play college ball. Most likely, fewer than one in 100 get a full athletic scholarship.

My last semester at Syracuse was my most rewarding— mainly because football was behind me. I got a glimpse of what school could really be like, especially in a seminar on Education and Society, taught by Hank Woessner, one of the few teachers I met who had faith in the students' ability to involve themselves in serious work. Hank was the first teacher to discuss in the classroom some of the problems I had been struggling with privately during my years at Syracuse. He constantly provoked us to question the whole concept of education. He talked about what education should be ideally and the reality at Syracuse. I began having long discussions with Hank about my role as a football player at Syracuse and the relationship of football to the rest of the university. With his encouragement, I wrote a term paper on the role of college football in higher education. The paper showed that big time college football was completely antithetical to the professed aims and goals of higher education, saying in a scholarly way what I had been feeling on a personal level since my junior year. For the first time it occurred to me that questioning the system was not something to feel guilty about, but a sane response.

6

Revolution in the Press Box

The revolt occurring in college athletics is not restricted solely to athletes. Just as there is a new social awareness developing among athletes, so the same thing is happening among sports writers. Until recently, most college sports writers restricted themselves to recording the exploits of their campuses' athletic stars and rubber stamping their athletic departments' policies. While a student at the University of California, I served as consulting sports editor for the school newspaper, and I still remember how upset and angry the athletic department's sports publicist was when he discovered that the Daily Cal's *sports staff was no longer going to serve as an extension of his office. Even after he admitted that he would not hesitate to try to suppress the truth if he felt it would hurt the athletic department's image, he could not understand why we viewed our interests as different from his and treated his press releases with some suspicion.*

Discrimination against blacks and women is just as rampant in the press box as it is on the playing field. In the few instances where women and blacks are found in press boxes, they are usually not there as members of the press, but as members of a staff hired to administer to the needs of the white male sports writers. The excuse given by newspaper editors for not hiring blacks or women is that they are unable to find qualified applicants. Consequently, if both sexism and racism are to be eliminated in the field of sports writing, college sports staffs must begin to make a diligent effort to recruit black and women writers. This is an essential step, for it is on college newspapers that most sports writers serve their apprenticeship.

Besides working to demythologize the sports world, the new breed of college sports writer is also attempting to dispel the stereotype image of all athletes as being crewcutted, dumb jocks. Unfortunately, whether it be on the high school, college, or professional level, athletes who speak out are almost always severely dealt with by their coaches and the sports establishment. In the spring of 1970, Robert Danielson, a seventeen year old baseball star at Del Valle High School in Walnut Creek, California, published a poem in his school's yearbook in which he poked fun at many of his fellow athletes who "don't reason" and "don't ask questions." Danielson's coach became infuriated and told him not to show up for his letter at a presentation award dinner. "I like the kid . . . I think he's pathetic but I like him," the coach commented. "If I hadn't, he wouldn't have played baseball for me for two years" (San Francisco Chronicle, *Wednesday, June 10, 1970, pg. 3). Fortunately, Danielson's high school athletic career was already completed when he published the poem, and all the coach could do was to refuse to award him his letter. Frank J. Salzhandler, an outstanding swimmer at the University of Texas, was not so fortunate as Danielson. Salzhandler chose to do some sports writing for the University of Texas school paper while he was still a member of the Texas swimming team. "All around the country," Salzhandler wrote, "athletes are beginning to seek meaning and relevance behind the work and dedication they put into athletics. When these ideas are stunted by a coach who only wants a group of bodies to lead around by the nose, many athletes are left with no alternative but to speak out" (San Francisco* Examiner, *Friday, October 23, 1970, pg. 56). Within twenty-four hours after his article was published in the school paper, Salzhandler was suspended from the team by the coach, Bill Patterson, who claimed his "attitude was intolerable and not conducive to winning" (San Francisco* Examiner, *Friday, Oct. 23, 1970, pg. 56).*

Despite this kind of pressure, an ever increasing number of college sports writers are themselves varsity athletes. Will Hetzel, recently a star basketball player at the University of Maryland, and Randy Smyth, a school record holder in track and field at the Uni-

WILL HETZEL, basketball player for the University of Maryland and one of the many college athletes who no longer fit the stereotype of the dumb, crew-cut, mumbling jock: "Playground games are so much more fun than college games. The people on the playground are playing primarily for the enjoyment of the physical activity, and that's what athletics should be all about. . . . Athletics can be such a beautiful thing. It's a shame to have to keep score. In fact, it's a shame to have to keep score on anything in life" (*Courtesy University of Maryland Athletic Department*).

*versity of California, are two individuals whose writing talents
match their athletic skill. A few of Randy Smyth's articles are reprinted here, along with some other articles that also appeared in
the* Daily Cal *during the spring of 1970. Not surprisingly, most of
these articles do not exhibit the objective, dispassionate style of
the professional sports writer, but this, rather than being a weakness, just might be their strength.*

WHERE WE'RE AT

BY LEWIS LEADER

It has been a custom for sports columnists and editors to be to
the right of Genghis Khan politically, and to be behind Spiro Agnew in insight.

Probably sleeping with red, white and blue covers, they have
usually agreed with one another that (1) Cassius Clay (usually
failing to call him Muhammad Ali) ought to be barred from boxing and sent to jail for all time, (2) athletes with long hair should
not be allowed to compete until shorn of their locks and shown the
wrongs of their ways, and (3) major critiques of the American
athletic system are inspired by kooks, Commies or creeps.

In the last few years, things have begun to change in the sports
section. Hopefully, this will continue. It is no longer necessary to
wear your American Legion or Veterans of Foreign Wars hat
while writing sports. In many newspaper offices, it still helps, however.

A sports section and its editor owe more to its readers than to
simply carry yesterday's scores, today's schedule and the standard
interview which often seems as if it was written by an awestruck
youngster meeting his hero for the first time.

Likewise, a college sports section must delve into the many issues concerning collegiate sports. There are many questions which
must be answered.

What is the relationship of the athletic department to the average student? Is the college coach the employer of his athletes (who
are then his workers) or is he a professor working with his students? How much do professional sports interfere with collegiate

athletics? Where do women fit in the college athletics? These are some of the questions which we will hope to answer before the end of the school year.

Perhaps the major issue which needs to be analyzed is the role of Third World athletes. Are they brought here to be exploited for four years for the glory of the school? Why are there so few Chicanos on Cal's teams? Can a Third World athlete find work with the athletic department if he wants it when his eligibility is used up?

The sports world must not sit back and watch everything go to pot all around it. It cannot, as some of its backers would prefer, exist in a vacuum unrelated to the world.

So must a college sports section find out what is going on underneath its own nose on its own campus. This is where we're at.

(*Mr. Leader served as sports editor of the* Daily Cal *during the spring of 1970.*)

SEX AND THE HIGH SCHOOL PROSPECT

by RANDY SMYTH

I remember when I got recruited. It was like being the most popular whore in town. Such stalwart academic institutions as Northern Arizona, New Mexico State and Brigham Young, just had to relay their sports wet dreams to me.

You can't imagine the sales-pitches the pesky coaches can hook you on. It's a mainliner to your ego the moment the flesh-hunting season opens. Some kids O.D. After talking with a few college recruiters, I didn't doubt for a minute that I was a twentieth century Achilles.

Most smart athletes tell the recruiters that they have preferences, and the state of Iowa is definitely out of the picture. But I had never been treated with such pomp, so I believed all they said. I mean, I thought they were calling me because they liked me.

And all those steak dinners. First he calls, from Illinois, and talks for over an hour. He tells me when he'll be by to meet the family. He comes by in his fresh-off-the-Hertz-lot red, air-conditioned, convertible Chevy. He unloads a suitcase full of junk literature and glossy pictures of his school. After a bone crushing handshake and a few cliches, we're off to a little steak house "down the road a piece" (they really talk like that).

Next comes the data about how U. of Tulsa is educationally comparable to Yale and Harvard. My mind drifts as we settle into another steak dinner. It's the third steak dinner of the week for me. Why not a pheasant, or Korean food, or a ham sandwich, or anything but steak. Such imagination.

After an unabashed statement about how Vanderbilt offers me an inside into the race for the Heisman Trophy (but coach, what about that guy O.J.?), the subject drifts to the topic of sex. That's always a sure one to land a recruit.

Without batting an eye, he tells me that if I choose Colorado State, I will never have another "lean moment."

"You mean I'll get, uh, find the girls, uh, they like athletes?"

"Son, at State the girls WORSHIP athletes."

"Gee, coach, that sounds great."

"Look, I'll put it this way, if you're ever going to get any action in your life, and you certainly look man enough, it'll be at State."

The use of sex in recruiting gets so heavy that the athletic departments at all schools know someone who knows someone who has a little red book of "dates" used to entice terribly horney young recruits. Every school I visited had a nice Aryan date waiting for me. At Louisiana State my date sounded like a public relations staff member.

Wichita State was not so subtle. Another recruit and I were each given a twenty dollar bill and a blind date. With a dirty grin and a "have fun," the coach sent us off in his red, air-conditioned, convertible Chevy. My date liked to tease me with little quips like "Oh, there's the motel—I mean theater."

Above and beyond all other institutions of higher learning, Berkeley came up with the best sales pitch. The date they got for me settled the issue of where I was going to school. I'm just lucky I didn't meet her at Northern Minnesota State. Strangely, the night seemed to end just as I got serious.

At two in the morning, standing at the doorstep of her sorority plantation, her arms wrapped gently around my trying-to-be-cool body, she whispered into my ears that she would be waiting to hear from me when I came back—permanently. The next few weeks were almost unbearable for me. The moment I reached Berkeley, I made my dream phone call.

"Hello, Jane . . . this is Randy."

"Uh, hi, Randy. . . . Randy who?"

(The use of coeds to entice star high school athletes to enroll at a particular college is not an uncommon practice. A few schools have even institutionalized this practice. Vince Gibson, the Kansas State football coach, proudly points out a picture of fifty beautiful Kansas coeds who help him recruit to most anyone who visits his office. He has dubbed them the "Gibson Girls," and will always explain how they are "hand-picked" from over three hundred candidates. At the University of Florida where the football team is known as the Gators, the coeds used for recruiting are referred to by the athletic department as the "Gator Getters.")

WILLSEY—COACH OR EDUCATOR?

BY TONY FOGLIANI AND JIM SMITH

Ray Willsey, Cal's head football coach, has declined to represent himself and his conservative coaching establishment with a free-handed two hour lecture.

To many students taking Education 191D (Intercollegiate Athletics and Higher Education), his refusal to speak to the class was only a manifestation of the incongruency of the role of athletics within an educational institution. This refusal convinced many students of the coach's inconsistent role as an educator.

Inasmuch as intercollegiate athletics exist under the pretense of being part of an academic curriculum (by having unit accreditation—with coaches supposedly being educators), why did Willsey decline to speak to the class? As an educator with a responsibility to students, were his reasons justifiable?

Willsey stated that he had to decline because the two hours between 8 and 10 P.M. on a Monday night would interfere with his recruiting of prospective football players. Should the recruiting of athletes be more important to Willsey, the educator, than his responsibility to the 400 students inquiring into the role of athletics at this university?

How often has Willsey been asked to present his views on athletics' role in a university?—once in his five years here at Cal—and then he declines. Possibly Willsey believes he cannot defend his position. Can it be presumed that he acknowledges that his role is not that of an educator, but that of a professional athletic bureaucrat whose primary responsibility is to produce winning teams?

By not appearing, Willsey is reinforcing many people's beliefs that his position in an academic institution is indefensible. But if his position is defensible and he can justify the position of the conservative coaching establishment, certainly a lecture to this class would be an excellent opportunity to present his views and correct any misconceptions or untruths that he feels are being generated by Scott and his class content.

In last week's lecture, three established coaches, Hal Connolly, George Davis, and Jim Klein, all with personal success and experience in the athletic world, demonstrated that an athletic endeavor can be an educational experience for the athlete without the coercion, incongruencies and hardships imposed on the athlete by most collegiate athletic directors and coaches.

These coaches showed that an individual athlete or a team can be successful without authoritarian discipline, imposed life styles and attitudes, and impositions upon academic careers.

Mr. George Davis, a highly successful football coach at St. Helena High School (45 wins, no losses 1961–1965), allows his players to determine starting line-ups by a democratic vote. He believes if athletics are to be educational, i.e., to create responsible and aware individuals who can make decisions in life and in society, then they must be given the power and freedom in athletics to begin developing the ability to make decisions democratically and behave responsibly.

Coaches like George Davis have indicated that reforms can occur within the archaic structure of football without destroying the game's appeal to either the athlete or spectator. The need is obvious: an alternate successful system is available; only the desire for honest reform is lacking.

(*Both Fogliani and Smith were football players at Cal. Ray Willsey was their coach.*)

A SPORTS CASUALTY

by RANDY SMYTH

Sadly, there is another sports casualty to report. No, it is not a pulled muscle or a broken heart from a lost race. This story is about a defeated person—another in the endless series of athletes getting crunched by the enterprise known as college athletics.

The latest casualty is Cal sprinter and former football player Jim Smith. Among his friends and coaches he was known as a "rebel" athlete because he asked too many questions. But this quarter, he could take no more. He quit sports and within a week he quit school and he split.

In talking with Jim the day before he left, I could relate to what he was saying and I recalled hearing the same sad story so many times from other athletes in the same cruel situation. An athlete gets bummed by the system which requires him to put in a 40-hour-week in sports while he receives just over $100 a month on a scholarship; of getting behind in school and then being forced to take useless classes to keep up his g.p.a. so he can stay in school to remain eligible for sports.

With few exceptions, the former college athletes I know are all "six-year men." Six years to graduate—hopefully. Don't show me your damn figures on how good it is; I've seen all kinds of data. Still I see my former teammates struggling through twenty units per quarter to finish in six years.

I don't want to hear of another goddamn star with a 3.0 g.p.a. I've talked with too many former jocks on dean's lists whose "junk class" 3.0 didn't help the guy get a degree. For every athlete who profited by sports, there are fifty who got screwed.

His departure from sports and education was begun when he started questioning the treatment of athletes in sports. His friends, his parents, everyone, told him how enviable his position in sports was.

But he knew he was getting overworked and his scholarship wasn't enough.

When he grew his hair long last season, the coach began to bug him a little; then a lot. The next thing he knew, he was called a "rebel"; in coaching jargon, he had an "attitude problem." He took this half-seriously, but the hair problem led to a confrontation and a threatened walk-out of last year's NCAA finals.

He carried his "rebel" attitude to the football team the next fall. First team flanker for a while, Jim questioned a decision of one of the coaches, and while still on the practice field was kicked off of the team—an unprecedented event. He then realized the price an athlete pays to compete—being bought by slave wages, being shortchanged in the classroom, and having his personality controlled by the coaches.

Jim had dreamed of going to graduate school, but few graduate schools in the country will accept someone with mediocre grades. In biology, without a higher degree, a bachelor's degree does not carry much weight. So he lost interest, quit school and split.

Talking with Jim saddened and made me so angry I could scream. I know so many athletes who have been crushed by it all. I know guys who got so shattered by the experience of sports and school that they wound up shooting smack within months.

As an athlete at Cal, your eligibility lasts only four years. It will be a lot longer than four years before the Athletic Establishment changes. If you open your mouth, you're put out. Jim Smith couldn't afford to open his mouth, but then, he couldn't afford not to.

"Come together"—John Lennon.

(*Jim Smith and Randy Smyth were teammates on the Cal track team for two years. They are both members of the school record-holding 440 relay team, a team that recorded the excellent time of 39.8.*)

SALT 'N PEPPER

BY RANDY SMYTH

In Cal's athletic sphere, there are no race relations. Black athletes hang around with blacks, eat with blacks, and room with blacks. White athletes hang around with whites, eat with whites, and room with whites.

On the athletic field, it is not much different. Blacks and whites are physically cast together for the practice sessions and games, but there is something lacking from real "me and you" conversations. When a black athlete and a white athlete talk, usually it is about sports, about coaches, maybe about school; but rarely do the conversations cover personal problems.

For the athletes, segregation and separation is much more striking off of the athletic field than it is on. Once the athletes are off the practice field, there is a change in attitude, both in coaches and athletes.

After practice, the coach is another person. He is buddy-buddy with everyone. The athletes change, too. After showering with the team—a somewhat equalizing experience in itself—the athletes are separate again; blacks walk away with blacks, and whites walk away with whites.

What people in general don't understand, and white athletes in particular, is that the athletic establishment plays on this total absence of communication. It blocks any attempt by a white athlete to try and reach across the abyss to find a black friend. It's okay for a black to try and be white, but for a white athlete to try and find out what is going on in the black athlete's head is not tolerated.

Accusations of this sort are difficult to prove because coaches and their bosses are very subtle. A compassionate white athlete is not called a "nigger lover" anymore, or even a "troublemaker." What is done is to block "it" before "it" starts. "It" is communication and it is blocked by the "psych" job on white athletes. The black and white communication gap must be quite important to the athletic department, or they would not try so hard to keep that gap in existence.

As a former athlete, I can recall the line of white athletes. Most were unconscious of the need for communication: all took the lack of communication for granted. When an issue would come up, no matter what, they would back the coach. He always seemed to be on the "white" side of an issue.

The white jocks were so inculcated with the coaches' position that they even began to use the rhetoric of the coaches and, when they became excited, it was hard to tell the difference between them and the coaches. Most white athletes I know of opposed the spring football boycott by the black athletes in 1968; no white athlete I know of participated in the Third World Strike in the winter of 1969.

It is no wonder then, that there is an absence of communication between black and white athletes. White athletes resemble the same oppressors who plague black athletes now; black athletes don't trust the whites. It is just what the athletic department wants. No communication—no problems.

But the black athletes at Cal do have very real problems—each categorically denied by the athletic department. If everything is so rosy for the black athletes on this campus, why did they feel the need to form the United Black Athletes?

White students and athletes must come to realize that racism is here, and that nowhere is it more obnoxious than in the brow-beating world of athletics. The first step is for white students and white athletes to come to an understanding of what the athletic department is doing. Then, and only then, will the communication between black and white athletes begin to reach the level which the athletic department is so desperately trying to prevent.

One of the most difficult problems college sports writers must face is what to do during a time of campus turmoil such as the period after the 1970 invasion of Cambodia and tragic killings at Kent State and Jackson State. Most athletic departments will invariably carry on with business as usual, but sports staffs need not do this. During a four-day period of daily battles between students and police on the Berkeley campus in the spring of 1970, the Daily Cal

*sports staff infuriated the athletic department by refusing to pub-
lish a "normal" sports page. The following article, written by
Sports Editor Lewis Leader, accompanied only by a picture of a
policeman guarding the gymnasium (see p. 78), is representative
of the* Daily Cal *sports page during this crisis.*

THURSDAY AFTERNOON—I am sitting up in the *Daily Cal*
sports department. Somehow, I just don't feel that I can report the
"happenings in the world of sports" as if nothing else is going on
on the campus. Because a hell of a lot is going on.

People are being gassed and clubbed. Tear gas and rocks are in
the air. There have been perhaps 50 arrests in two days. Dozens of
people have been injured. The entire campus is in a state of turmoil. As I write this I can see police pushing a student into a win-
dow on the terrace. Chancellor Heyns has made his usual statement, and declared the campus to be in a "state of emergency."
Sproul Hall has closed its first floor offices for the day. The San
Francisco Symphony scheduled to play at King Hall Thursday
night has postponed its performance. Yet, the athletic department
has decided to continue on with its full schedule of athletic events.

The sports world has almost always continued on its own way,
oblivious to the events of the country. Sports are considered to be
an integral part of American society. Yet, when events affect that
society, the sports world wants to continue as if nothing happened.

When President Kennedy was assassinated, National Football
League Commissioner Pete Rozelle decided to go ahead with the
full schedule of NFL games on the Sunday following the Friday as-
sassination. The reasoning was that the country needed something
to turn to in that time of national tragedy. But many people, including many of those who had to play, felt that it wasn't the time
to turn their thoughts away from what had happened.

"I really felt a tremendous revulsion to playing, and I think
many of the ball players felt the same way," Dave Meggyesy of the
St. Louis Cardinals told me this afternoon, about playing that day.
Meggyesy said that in talking with other ball players the majority
opinion was that the game should be postponed, possibly to the
end of the season.

When Martin Luther King was assassinated in April of 1968,

This picture, along with the concluding article in Chapter 6, was all that appeared on the sports page of the Daily Californian the day after a particularly violent battle between police and students during an anti-ROTC demonstration (*Photo courtesy Jim Yudelson*).

Walter O'Malley, then president of the Los Angeles Dodgers, said that the scheduled league opener with the Philadelphia Phillies would be played. Finally, after the Phillies said that they would forfeit rather than play the game, the game was postponed.

Likewise, when Robert Kennedy was assassinated only two months later, there were those familiar lines like "Bobby would have wanted the games to be played."

Here at Cal, the sports world is going to continue with its full slate of events—crew, baseball and tennis here, track and field and golf away. More than one athlete is not happy with this. However, because they know they face the possibility of severe punishment if they don't participate, they are faced with difficult personal choices.

There are many of you who will feel that the sports page is abrogating its responsibility to the sports world because you will not find normal sports coverage in today's paper. But things are not normal on this campus. Anyone can see that. The least we can do is stop and think about what has been going on on this campus. If we choose to ignore what is happening, we work to perpetuate the problems. We cannot adopt a "business as usual" attitude by pretending nothing is wrong, as those who keep athletic events going have chosen to do.

If the sports world wants to continue on as if it is operating in a vacuum, it will. But I don't live in a vacuum.

7

The Revolt of the
Black Athlete

Much of the turmoil in high school and college athletics over the past few years has been the result of conflicts between white coaches and black athletes. Few schools have been unaffected by these conflicts, and on well over 100 college campuses overt disruptions have occurred. Because of these conflicts, many college coaches and athletic directors are privately, and sometimes even publicly, discussing the possibility of no longer recruiting black athletes. As one nationally prominent track coach told me, "Unless we can find a way to separate the decent ones from the troublemakers and militants, we're going to stop recruiting all Negroes."

The revolt of black athletes, which began in earnest during 1968 and is still gathering momentum, caught the white American sports establishment completely off guard. It was caught off guard because it mistakenly assumed that the docility and acquiescence common in Negro athletes of the past was an inherent quality rather than a posture Negroes had adopted as the only way to survive in a racist sports world. Conditions have improved for the black athlete as we enter the 1970's, but his protests have not been abated, and this is what infuriates the white sports establishment. Not surprisingly, the oppressor's perspective is not the same as that of the oppressed: whites want to emphasize how much conditions have improved for the black athlete over the years, while the black athlete who still experiences daily the effects of racism is not so concerned with how much better things are, but with how bad they still are.

Until the latter half of the 1960's, almost all Negro athletes labored under the premise that they could best help themselves and their people by keeping their mouths shut and proving their prowess on the athletic field. Consequently, from the coach's perspective, most Negro athletes were ideal pupils. The racist stereotype of the Negro athlete as a malingerer was simply not true. Sport was one of the few avenues where the Negro was given any chance at all, and for most Negro athletes, sports dominated their lives. They obediently and smilingly went through their paces, jumping at their white coaches' every command. Their goal—as defined by the white man—was to be a credit to their race.

White society told the Negro he could prove his humanity by accomplishments in the athletic arena, but when Negroes began to dominate many sports, white coaches such as Dean Cromwell, the legendary University of Southern California track coach, reversed themselves and claimed, ". . . the Negro excels in the events he does because he is closer to the primitive than the white man. It was not long ago that his ability to sprint and jump was a life-and-death matter to him in the jungle" (1941, p. 6). First the white racists accused Negroes of being too inferior to accomplish anything significant in sports, and then when Negroes demonstrated their competence, the racists claimed these accomplishments proved their inferiority! This was the kind of Catch-22 world the Negro athlete lived in until recently—nothing he could do was quite good enough. No matter what he accomplished, the white sports establishment would not grant him his humanity.

Until recently, the Negro athlete with a social conscience could honestly believe he was helping his people as well as himself by devoting all his energies to improving himself as an athlete. Today, it is difficult to imagine that there are any Negro athletes so naïve. The Negro athlete who gives his entire being to sport is now usually viewed as being selfish and only concerned with his own advancement. It is athletes such as Bill Russell and Tommie Smith who have combined athletic accomplishment with social commitment who are the sport heroes in the black community. There are even an ever increasing number of outstanding black athletes who are giving up promising athletic careers entirely in order to work full-time in the black liberation struggle (San Francisco *Chronicle,* June 22, 1970, p. 50).

After years of coaching Negro athletes whose entire lives centered around athletics, most white coaches simply cannot understand what has happened. His grinning, obedient Negro athletes have turned into proud black athletes, and the coach is scared. In fact, the entire sports establishment is so frightened that the NCAA *News,* the official organ of the NCAA, in December of 1969 came out with an editorial that attempted to give the impression that there is no real legitimacy to the revolts of black college athletes that are breaking out on campuses all over the country. Quite understandably, attacks such as this only confirm in the minds of most black athletes their feelings about the racist nature of the white sports establishment.

White coaches are upset that black athletes now have other things on their minds besides running and jumping, and an increasing number of coaches are demanding that black athletes sign pledges agreeing to give 100 per cent effort to their college's athletic program. Black athletes who refuse to sign these pledges are denied the opportunity to participate in intercollegiate athletics. Many black athletes believe that to sign such a pledge would be a betrayal of the black liberation struggle; they feel the coach is asking them to make everything secondary to sports, and they are unwilling to do this. The white coach on the other hand, going on the basis of years of experience with earlier generations of Negro athletes, feels he is making a perfectly reasonable request. If the white coaches who are demanding that black athletes sign these pledges would honestly try to communicate with the black athletes, they would discover that the athletes' refusal to sign the pledges does not necessarily indicate anything about their desire to participate in sports. Black athletes simply feel that it is an insult to themselves and the black liberation struggle for a coach to demand that they publicly declare that their most important concern is the success of their school's athletic program.

A conflict which reveals the nature of many of the problems between white coaches and black athletes developed on the University of California track team during the spring of 1969. The central figures in this conflict were a white coach who had a history of problems with black athletes and the black captain of the track team, a young man who had a deep commitment to the black liberation struggle. The conflict began when the track season was still weeks away, and while a student strike was in progress on the Cal campus. The student strike was led by third world students, and they had called for a student boycott of classes and all university activities after all other peaceful means had failed in their attempt to get a Third World College instituted on the campus.

The black athletes on the track team supported the strike, and they informed Sam Bell, the head track coach, that they would not be able to come to practice or compete in any meets if the season began while the strike was still in progress. Coach Bell listened to the black athletes explain their position and then informed them that their scholarships would not be renewed and that they would be permanently barred from the team unless they immediately returned to practice at the regular track under his supervision. At this point, the blacks offered a compromise solution; they agreed to train daily at a local high school track under the supervision of an assistant coach and promised to rejoin the team as soon as the strike was settled. But Bell would not compromise; his ultimatum stood.

Even though the season had not begun and track is not a team sport that requires athletes to train together, Bell put the black athletes in the position where they had to choose between competing in track or supporting their fellow students in the strike. Most, but not all, of the black athletes returned to the team. One of the black athletes who continued to honor the strike was Stanley Royster, an All-American in the long jump the preceding year. Royster had placed first in 14 of the 15 dual meets he had competed in for Cal, and because of his athletic ability and quiet inspirational leadership, his teammates had elected him captain of the team. He explained that he felt a responsibility to the track team, but that he felt an even greater responsibility to his people.

The white sports establishment frequently attempts to discredit black athletes such as Royster by claiming that they are nothing but troublemakers who have no real desire to participate

STANLEY ROYSTER, NCAA All-American in the long jump and captain of the 1969 University of California track team. Royster was dismissed from the Cal track team when he became actively involved in the black liberation struggle on the Berkeley campus (*Photo courtesy Jack Scott*).

in sports. This accusation often seems to be true, but it is only because when an athlete is kicked off a college team he usually has no team he can compete for and is thus forced to stop competing. Track and field, however, is one sport where an athlete can often manage to continue competing even after being dismissed from his school's team. Royster continued competing after being barred from the Cal team, and only a few weeks later he had the longest jump of his career. The next year, 1970, he placed 4th in the National AAU Championships.

Stanley Royster is representative of the new type of black athlete developing in the United States. He, like so many other black athletes, has demonstrated that social commitment is not necessarily antithetical to athletic accomplishment. Black athletes like Royster, who are demanding they be treated with dignity, are having conflicts with white coaches, not because they are unwilling to perform on the playing field, but simply because white coaches do not like their attitude. For those white coaches who are so racist that they are incapable of treating black athletes with dignity, conflicts and disruptions have only just begun. However, there are some white coaches who are honestly trying to make a new beginning, and a necessary first step for these coaches is to realize that social commitment and athletic accomplishment are not mutually exclusive.

8

Black Power at Mexico City*

"The untypical exhibitionism of these athletes . . . violates the basic standards of sportsmanship which are highly regarded in the United States," said Bob Paul, press officer of the U.S. Olympic Committee. He was attempting to explain why the Committee had just suspended black sprinters Tommie Smith and John Carlos from the American team.

After rough going at the press conference, Paul walked over to an unfriendly reporter and asked to see his credentials. The credentials were from *Ramparts*. "You're on the niggers' side, aren't you?" he said.

But this was to be expected: the U.S. Olympic Committee was scared. On October 16, 1968, when Smith and Carlos stood on the victory stand after the 200 meter dash, their gold and bronze medals resting on their chests, their gloved fists raised defiantly and their heads bowed as America's national anthem was played, the U.S. Olympic Committee realized that it was no longer the sole spokesman for the U.S. Olympic team. For when the music stopped, Smith and Carlos looked up to the 80,000 people in the stadium and in unison slowly turned full circle, their fists still raised. There was a thin chorus of boos from some American spectators, but as the large majority of Mexicans in the crowd realized what they were witnessing, they cheered and applauded.

When the Committee got around to suspending Smith and

* A similar version of this article, co-authored by myself and Robin Cochran, originally appeared in *Ramparts* magazine, November 30, 1968.

Carlos thirty hours later, it was too late. They were already heroes —not for most of the American press, of course, but for the black and brown athletes from all over the world. Not even the elaborate public relations machinery at the disposal of Avery Brundage and his cohorts could change that. Mexican kids were chasing John Carlos all over town, begging for his autograph; the Jamaican team came to the American athletes' lodging to offer support and to ask what they could do to help. The Cubans came around to offer their congratulations and to extend an invitation to Smith and Carlos to visit their country. Later, the superb Cuban 400 meter relay team sent its silver medals to Harry Edwards.

A feeling of solidarity began to form at the XIX Olympiad among black athletes of the whole world. It was not anti-white, but anti-racist. "We're all related," said Kenyan Daniel Rudisha, "and we all have a cause to run for here."

There were plenty of white athletes, including many on the American team, who took Smith and Carlos' side in the affair. Hal Connolly and Ed Burke, hammer throwers on the U.S. team, both added their voices to those of the blacks on the team who threatened to withdraw from the Games after the suspension. Wearing the button of Harry Edwards' organization, the "Olympic Project for Human Rights" (which he had obtained from Lee Evans), Martin Jellinghaus, the spokesman for the bronze medal winning West German 1600 meter relay team, said: "I am wearing this medal because I feel solidarity not only for them as persons, but for the movement, the human rights movement." Peter Norman, an Australian sprinter who shared the victory stand with Smith and Carlos, also wore one, and was reprimanded by the moguls on the Australian Olympic Committee. And the Harvard crew team that had publicly declared their support for the Olympic Project for Human Rights was constantly harassed by Olympic officials. In fact, as late as the evening before the finals of their competition, the Harvard crew did not know for certain whether U.S. Olympic officials would allow them to compete.

The day after Smith and Carlos' demonstration, the black and brown athletes who were not competing crowded into Section 22 of the stadium, the focus of a great deal of activity for the remainder of the track and field events. Every time a black athlete won an event, Section 22 responded with a clenched fist salute, and the athlete on the field would return the gesture. "This fist," said Carlos, "signifies the coming together of people who've been apart for a long time." The Africans, like Kip Keino, winner at 1500 meters over America's Jim Ryun, answered Section 22 not with a fist but with one finger raised for "first." Madeline Manning, a young black woman from Cleveland, won the 800 meters, and Section 22 went wild. Two competitors from the Bahamas set up a rhythm on conga drums, and the Africans chanted in time with the music. John Carlos danced up and down the aisles. It was pure joy, and somehow each victory became a vindication of Smith and Carlos.

The U.S. Olympic Committee, ABC television, and most American sports writers toted up the United States' medals and compared them to the Russians', as has been their custom since the Soviets first entered the Games in 1952 and brought them within the realm of the Cold War. But in Mexico City, some people added up new figures: black versus white. In men's track and field, the score was 12 to 9 in favor of the blacks. Admittedly, such figures, any figures, are not in harmony with the Olympic ideal, but these tactics were begun by men—and they were not black men—who have used the Games for their own political purposes for a long time now.

And even as Section 22 was basking in the performance of the black athletes, there were some U.S. coaches keeping statistics for themselves and making their own judgments. "As far as Carlos goes, I was hoping that he wouldn't even place," said Jim Bush, UCLA track coach and reportedly one of those being considered for Payton Jordan's job as head coach of the American team. "They want everything, they want the world. They don't want the Olympics, they want everything given to them."

The blacks in the 1968 Olympic Games didn't need to have anything given to them. They took it.

9

Amateurism: A Needed Revision

Though this chapter specifically addresses itself to the question of amateurism in one sport, track and field, the issues and problems examined here are by no means unique to track and field. In recent years, nearly every amateur sport has altered, or at least begun to question, its approach to amateurism. Basing my argument on the assumption that sport should be conducted primarily for the benefit of participating athletes, I point out the discriminatory nature of existing amateur regulations and offer suggestions for the development of a humane, just code.

The winners of the track and field events in Rome [1960 Olympic Games] this year will, almost every one of them, have trained at least two hours a day for at least two years. None of these, unless he has private means, can have done that, and travelled over the world to get the necessary competition, and at the same time have remained in any meaningful sense of the word an amateur.

CHRIS CHATAWAY (1960)

The problem of amateurism is one where at first glance I find my heart in one place and my head in another. I agree and sympathize with many of the ideals of amateurism, especially as they are outlined by Dr. J. Kenneth Doherty, retired University of Pennsylvania track and field coach (1965, pp. 3–8). Doherty, whose books on track and field are probably the finest ever written by an American, has an authentic love for the innate beauty and goodness of track and field, and he believes that these precious qualities of sport can only be preserved by a return to "pure" amateurism. And since I disagree with the reasoning behind one of the main arguments against amateurism—this being the idea that since sports are a vehicle for international prestige, we should relax amateur regulations so we can keep up with the Soviet bloc countries*—I have always been an admirer of those individuals who fought to keep track and field free of any taint of professionalism.

Yet, when athletes and sports writers all over the world are calling for changes in the existing amateur code, I cannot help but wonder if it is not possible to protect the ideals Doherty admires while, at the same time, revise the amateur code so that it will be in accord with contemporary conditions. Those individuals calling for change are every bit as interested in the welfare of track and field and the well-being of individual athletes as Doherty, and they certainly would not advocate change if they felt this would be detrimental.

Ideals, in their detachment from the humdrum business of everyday existence, are a source of inspiration and guidance for man in his journey through life; but for an ideal to have any meaningful effect it must have a certain congruence with reality. Chastity is an ideal to some; but, since it is not in accord with man's nature, it is at worst a pernicious ideal and at best a foolish one. Those individuals who call for a return to the ideals of "pure" amateurism are as out of tune with reality as those well-meaning but misguided idealists who advocate sexual abstinence. Doherty will be as successful in getting athletes to follow his code of "pure" amateurism as Gandhi was in getting his followers to remain chaste.

A proper amateur code will serve to inspire and guide athletes while, at the same time, it will take into account certain facts of human existence. It will be enforceable; it will be in agreement with man's nature; and it will be fair and just for all nations and all ath-

* Ironically, those same individuals who are quick to condemn the Soviets are often the first to ape them.

letes. An amateur code—in order to be worthy of man's respect —must meet all three of these criteria.

PURE AMATEURISM?

Since Doherty offers what I believe to be the most intelligent, inspiring argument for "pure" amateurism, I will examine the principles he emphasizes and see how they measure up against our three criteria.

1. "In order to ensure fair competition, amateur sportsmen must agree to a certain limitation in time and energy that can properly be devoted to sports preparation" (Doherty, 1965, p. 6). This is a most reasonable proposal, for if we are to have true amateurism, the most equitable principle would be a world-wide limitation on the number of hours an athlete could train each week— all amateur athletes would be limited to say one and a half hours of training daily. Although performance standards might be lowered, competition would be just as keen, and many athletes who are presently forced to give up competitive sport because of the pressure of other obligations would be able to continue participating.

Yes, it all sounds very good—too good. The principle is an ideal that is not rooted in reality; it is unenforceable. And even if it were enforceable, it is questionable whether someone who is willing to make the necessary sacrifices to train more than ninety minutes a day—even though he may be employed at a legitimate job —should be denied that right. Great athletes always have been willing to make the necessary sacrifices in order to do sufficient training—Zatopek got in extra workouts by running in place for over an hour at a time while reading—and this principle would strike a blow at the very finest athletes: the Kutses, Elliotts, Whitfields, Snells, Shrubbs, Evanses, and the many future athletic greats. Champions will make every sacrifice they possibly can in order to actualize their full potential, and they should be praised for this, not condemned. This principle is not only unenforceable, for it would necessitate a twenty-four-hour-a-day watch on amateur athletes throughout the world, but it also is opposed to the nature of our finest athletes. Additionally, it doesn't apply equally to all countries: ninety minutes of sprint training on a muddy track in England is certainly not equivalent to ninety minutes on a Tartan track in sunny California. Quite clearly, this is a principle that does not merit serious consideration for inclusion in any future amateur code.

2. "A true amateur in sports, then, is one who has major work to do, not related to his sport, which requires a major portion of his time, his energy, and his interest. . . . How much time is required by a full-time vocation? Obviously the answers will vary greatly. Certainly it cannot be stated as a specific number of hours. But each vocation knows its own full-time requirements" (Doherty, 1965, p. 7). This principle could be enforceable—although not without some difficulty—and it is not opposed to man's nature. However, it does not apply equally and justly to all nations and all individuals. A full-time vocation in an underdeveloped country frequently demands a sixty-hour work week, while full-time employment in an advanced industrial nation seldom requires more than forty hours. This disparity will grow even larger in future years with the advance of automation.

Doherty, as part of his full-time vocation principle, mentions, "A true amateur in sports, then, is one who has major work to do *not related to his sport* . . ."* (1965, p. 7). Most athletes by personal inclination will prefer to earn their livelihood in activities unrelated to sport, but is it fair to say that Gordon Pirie, one of the world's outstanding distance runners, cannot make his living teaching athletics to young boys and girls if he wants to continue competing in track? If someone loves sports enough to make it his life's work, he should not be punished and banned from amateur competition as Pirie was. It is sensible and understandable that many athletes will choose to make their living teaching athletics, and it is most unreasonable to deny them this opportunity.

Gordon Pirie has a passionate love for athletics, and David Sime, not long ago a world record holding sprinter, has a similar love for medicine. Was it any more natural for Sime to become a neuro-surgeon than for Pirie to become an athletics teacher? Any principle that would deny athletes free choice of employment is not

* Emphasis mine.

worthy of man's respect and certainly does not warrant inclusion in a just amateur code.

A final amateur regulation pertaining to finances that merits discussion is the rule prohibiting athletes from capitalizing on their fame. This regulation runs into problems of enforceability—who is to say that Mary Rand would not have been a sports clothing model even if she had not won a gold medal at the Tokyo Games —but even more significantly, it does not have the same effect on all amateur athletes.

During the late nineteenth and early twentieth centuries, all but a few exceptional athletes such as Walter George and Alfred Shrubb trained only five or six hours a week. No doubt some athletes did this what we, today, would term light training because of personal laziness, but most athletes trained in this manner because they honestly believed any more training would "burn them out" and be detrimental to top performance. Zatopek, with his phenomenal training sessions, once and for all exposed this myth; and today we see many athletes training two, three, and four, and even five hours daily, six or seven days a week. Ron Clarke often does more training in one day than an old-time great like Joe Binks did in two weeks! And Clarke keeps this training up fifty-two weeks a year, whereas Binks took off a few months annually in order to guard against "staleness." There always will be athletes who yearn to perform as near to their maximum potential as possible; and now that it is recognized that increased training loads can facilitate them in this quest, an ever increasing number of athletes are spending unusually long hours training.

The groundwork has now been laid for showing how the principle of not capitalizing on one's athletic fame does not have the same effect on all athletes. Excluding athletic scholarship holders, state-employed athletes, and other athletes who also are presently violating this regulation, only financially independent athletes are able to spend the time on athletics that it takes to fully actualize their potential. This observation is substantiated by Chris Chataway's comment in the introductory quotation to this essay. Chataway, twice a British Olympian as well as a former world record holder in both the 5000 meters and three mile, believes that "None of these [Olympic medal winners at the Rome Games], unless he has private means, can have done that [the necessary training], and at the same time have remained in any meaningful sense of the word an amateur" (1960, pp. 51–52). If the existing Olympic and amateur codes had been enforced at Mexico City, essentially the entire United States Olympic track and field team, along with the teams of most other major countries, would have been barred from participation.

PURE AMATEURISM: A LUXURY ONLY THE WEALTHY CAN AFFORD

Amateur regulations were established in the late nineteenth century by wealthy aristocratic gentlemen primarily to keep them from having to compete against their social inferiors, men who often took sport seriously. Some might argue that it was not the conscious intent of the founders of the amateur code to bar all athletes from amateur competition who were not aristocrats, but few will deny that this was what happened when these regulations were instituted. All of the late nineteenth century and early twentieth century distance running greats such as Deerfoot, Walter George, and Alfred Shrubb were either professionals to begin with or were declared professionals for alleged violations of amateur rules.

"Pure" amateurism is a luxury that only the wealthy can afford. This becomes especially clear when we look at the men and women who usually get to the top in amateur sports that require expensive equipment as well as long periods of time in training. United States Olympic competitors in water sports such as swimming, rowing, and yachting are invariably white and almost always wealthy. Even track and field, one of the more egalitarian Olympic sports, is not immune from this kind of discrimination based on wealth and social position. Bill Toomey, because of his financial circumstances, was able to buy the best athletic equipment, travel throughout the world seeking the finest competition and coaching, and spend as much time as necessary training for a four or five year period in order to become the world's best decathlon man. Toomey was able to afford amateurism, but there are many equally talented, equally dedicated decathlon men who cannot. Unlike Toomey, they must regularly work at full-time jobs in order to make a living, and they cannot afford to purchase the equipment, drugs, and food supplements that he did, never mind travel around the world looking for competent coaching.[1]

One of the main reasons most officials and administrators are resistant to revising antiquated, class discriminatory amateur regulations is that these regulations give them wide-reaching control over all amateur athletes. Since almost every "amateur" is a violater of these regulations in one way or another, officials can ban —or at least threaten to ban—most any athlete who arouses their anger. This happened at the Mexico City Olympics where most of the top track and field athletes received anywhere from $500 to $8000 for wearing a particular brand of track shoe. It is difficult to imagine that American and international Olympic officials were not aware of the true extent of these "illegal" payments; yet, when they handed out their accusations, the only individuals mentioned were certain black Americans—athletes who not so incidentally had used the Games as a platform to protest racial injustice in the United States.

Top track and field athletes were receiving "under-the-table" payments long before the Mexico City Olympics. These payments are most common during the winter indoor circuit in the United States and during the summer European season. Many track "insiders" still talk about the great indoor 600 yard runner who, during the 1950's, demanded and usually got $1 per yard. When one prominent meet promoter saw fit to pay this individual only $500, our enterprising athlete went out and led the race at a blistering pace, but at the 500 yard mark he suddenly stepped off the track. He later insisted to inquiring sports writers and an irate meet promoter that he had felt a slight twinge in his hamstring and stopped

---

1. Toomey is unquestionably a great athlete, and since we were once training partners, I know the tremendous struggle that he had to go through to develop into a world record holder and Olympic champion. Bill had the courage to endure and keep struggling when nearly everyone had given up on him as a guy who just couldn't make it big. Still, in fairness to his fellow athletes, it should be recognized that it was his financial circumstances that gave him the opportunity to fully develop his potential.

in order to prevent a serious injury. From then on he always got his $600.

For years amateur officials have turned their heads while athletes who were in their good graces competed in U.S. indoor and European outdoor meets, pulling down thousands of dollars. It is common knowledge in track circles that over the past few years one of the world's top distance runners has been making well over $15,000 per summer on the European and Scandanavian circuits. Since this athlete's personal appearance and behavior reflect the conservative values of most amateur officials, he has never been rebuked for accepting "illegal" payments. However, when some top American athletes who have the reputation among amateur officials of being "radicals" or "militants" went to Europe during the summers of 1969 and 1970 expecting to make some money, they were quickly censored.

Sometimes the political control amateur regulations give officials over the lives of athletes takes an even less subtle form. As Harry Edwards and I pointed out in an article in the November, 1969, issue of *Ramparts* magazine, one prominent AAU official has offered money to black athletes in exchange for their agreeing to "look and behave like good Americans." Amateur and Olympic officials were infuriated by the protests of black athletes at the Mexico City Olympics, and these bribes are an attempt to insure that there will not be a repeat performance at the 1972 Games. But much to the consternation of amateur officials, most black athletes have chosen dignity over money. It is primarily because of this extensive political control amateur regulations give officials over the lives of amateur athletes rather than any concern for the "ideals" of amateurism that officials are reluctant to reform the existing code.

A PARTICIPANT OR SPECTATOR ORIENTATION

The cardinal virtue of amateur athletics is that since athletes are not paid for competing, the activity is more likely to maintain a *participant orientation* rather than a *spectator orientation*. H. A. Harris elaborates on this argument in his authoritative book, *Greek*

Athletes and Athletics. "So long as a sport is true to itself, the only purpose of the organization of it is the enjoyment of the players; as soon as the interests of the spectators are allowed to become predominant, corruption has set in and the essence of the game has been lost" (1964, p. 189). The *essence* of athletics (participation) is more important than the *accident* (spectator viewing). Once athletes are paid for competing in a country with a private-profit economy, the accident will usually become the essence, for the prime concern now is for the owner(s) to make a profit, and this is done by attracting spectators and landing lucrative radio and television contracts. The activity is then no longer conducted primarily for the benefit of the athletes, but for the owners to make a profit. And if past experience with other sports is any indication, owners will do whatever is necessary to make their profit.

If professionalism were introduced into American track and field, and athletes began getting paid for competing, commercialism would become even more rampant than it already is. Meet promoters would start using gimmicks such as the "Devil-Take-the-Hindmost Mile," an event popularized at the San Francisco *Examiner* Indoor Track and Field Meet. This race is run on a 160 yard, 11 laps to the mile, indoor track. After the first two laps of the race, the athlete in last place as the runners pass by the starting pole is required to drop out. Not surprisingly, in an effort not to be last, the runners start out running at a suicidal pace. Most fans love it, for, among other reasons, there is invariably a mad scramble by the runners at the rear of the pack every time they near the starting pole after the second lap since none of them want to pass this mark in last place and be forced out of the race. Normally one of the most rewarding aspects of track and field is that a runner, though finishing fifth or sixth—or even last for that matter—can still get tremendous satisfaction from having recorded a personal best or a time that was an accomplishment for him given his present level of conditioning. In the "Devil-Take-the-Hindmost Mile," most runners do not even get the chance to finish. And those who do finish, usually run a time much slower than they are capable of, since they had to run the first part of the race at such an extremely fast pace. Events like this one, and others promoters could dream up, stimulate and amuse unknowledgable fans, thus expanding potential audience size; but, more significantly, they destroy the innate beauty and nobility of track and field.

Over the past few years, a number of groups have made attempts to professionalize track and field. Almost all of them have tried to gain initial funding by securing lucrative television contracts. Track and field athletes and coaches, before allowing their sport to become anymore involved with television than it already is, might profit by looking at the problems surfers have encountered with TV.

Not too many years ago, the major television networks began showing documentaries on surfing. These programs received such a high audience rating that a decision was made to televise surfing contests live. This meant that the contests had to be held on a specific site at a prearranged time and date. Regardless of the weather conditions and, even more important, the condition of the surf, the surfers had to begin surfing when the television crews gave the signal. As you can probably well imagine, this caused some rather ludicrous and pathetic contests. By 1969, television and other forms of commercialism in surfing had gotten so out of hand that Wayne Lynch, an Australian who is regarded by many experts as the world's greatest surfer, refused to enter a single contest. As one American surfer told me, "Television is destroying our sport. The TV producers are turning a sport and an art form into a circus.[2]

2. Surfers, many of whom have a deeper involvement and commitment to their sport than athletes in most other sports, have recently begun to do something as a group about the commercialism and frequent mismanagement of surfing. Many of them are lobbying to have surfing contests scheduled over a week's period. Each morning, the surfers would gather at the beach and vote on whether they felt the conditions were appropriate for the contest to begin. If the vote was negative, they would meet for another vote in the early afternoon. This process would be repeated until a "yes" vote was obtained. If a good surf had not come up during the seven-day period, the contest would be cancelled. Other surfers are asking that they have the right to select the men and women who will judge their contests. They have made this request, for they feel that many of the older judges do not understand recent trends in surfing and, on more than one occasion, have discriminated against, "hippie-looking" surfers. It is encouraging to see athletes who love their sport to such an

Some of the problems that have sprung up with the televising of amateur track and field meets over the past few years give only a slight indication of what might occur if track and field became professionalized. Because of live television coverage, the starts of races have been delayed as long as half an hour. This works a great physical and mental hardship on athletes who are warmed up and ready to compete on schedule. Live coverage can also prove especially dangerous for distance runners when they are required to compete at a specific time regardless of weather conditions. It is neither healthy nor enjoyable to run six miles in the middle of a hot summer day, and competing at this time is certainly not conducive to the distance runners performing at their best. Yet, because of commercial interests and insensitive officials, American distance runners have been required to compete under these conditions.

Television coverage of track and field, even when not live, has created some major problems. In 1968 the AAU National Men's Track and Field Championship Meet, normally scheduled over a weekend, was shifted to Thursday and Friday at the request of ABC so that they could televise the highlights of the meet that weekend. Among other things, this worked a special hardship on employed athletes who were forced to take off two to three days from work in order to compete in the championships.[3]

---

extent that they will willingly give up money and publicity in order to preserve it as a means for creative self-expression.

I would like to thank Michael Salter who, in a term paper for a course I taught at the University of California at Berkeley, first made me aware of these significant developments in the surfing world.

3. In 1968 the AAU signed a lucrative contract with ABC giving them permission to televise major AAU track and field meets, including the national championships. Because of their own regulations prohibiting payment to amateurs, the AAU, of course, did not share the revenue received from the television contract with competing athletes. The athletes, besides laboring for free, also were required to take off two or three days from their jobs when the AAU agreed to ABC's demand that the meet be switched to Thursday and Friday.

This kind of rapacious behavior is nothing new to the AAU. Their greed for money and, often times, callous disregard for athletes were exhibited at least as early as 1936. Within a month after the Berlin Olym-

One can only imagine what would happen if track and field were professionalized and the television industry had an even larger financial stake in it than it has at present. What gimmicks and maneuvers would television producers resort to if audience ratings dropped and profits began to decline? Quite obviously, their prime concern would not be the athletes' welfare. If ABC could make a profit doing it, I believe they would take Jesse Owens out of retirement and have him once again race against horses as he did at the end of his career.

As a track and field coach and a former track athlete, I, and I'm sure most people in our sport, welcome the televising of track and field meets. However, it should be made clear to the television networks that the meet is not being conducted for their convenience, but primarily for the benefit of the competing athletes. The televising of a meet should, in no way, be allowed to interfere with the athletes' participation.

A POSITIVE CODE

The most intelligent, straightforward proposal for revision of the present code that I have come across in a review of the literature published on this topic is one offered by Dorothy Hyman, silver medalist over 100 meters at the Rome Olympics, in her autobiography *Sprint to Fame* (1964, p. 118).

I would hate to see athletes running for appearance or prize-money. I would detest seeing athletics meetings in the atmosphere of

pic Games, the AAU barred Jesse Owens, the hero of those Games, from amateur athletics solely because he refused to run in some Scandanavian track meets in which the AAU demanded he compete. Tired from racing almost daily for over a month since the end of the Berlin Olympics, in which he won four gold medals, Owens decided to come back to the United States for a well deserved rest. The AAU was furious and barred him, for—without Owens' permission—they had signed a contract with Scandanavian meet promoters guaranteeing Owens' presence at their meets. Larry Snyder, Owens' track coach at Ohio State, accused the AAU of treating Owens and other Olympic athletes like cattle. In a story in the August 18, 1936 New York *Times,* Snyder was quoted as saying, "There was no need for the suspension. . . . Down with Owens, the AAU says, because he refuses to help them swell their bank account. The boys merely are cattle being shipped about. Such things wouldn't occur and couldn't occur if greed on the part of the AAU were more easily satiated."

a dog track. . . . If running were professionalised I don't think I would have competed. I've always run because I loved it.

I don't believe in taking money out of athletics at all; only from commercial undertakings outside it. In other words, while I would never want to earn money by winning I would be all in favour of profiting through the various offers that can come as a RESULT of winning: appearing on TV, writing, modelling, endorsing sports equipment, advertising, selling and so on. I don't for a moment believe such earnings would interfere with the spirit of athletics: on the contrary, I'm sure the sport would benefit.

This proposal would not interfere with the present participant orientation of track; yet, it would give most athletes throughout the world—regardless of their private financial resources—the opportunity to fully develop their athletic potential. It is a very simple proposal that would present minimal enforcement problems. *Amateur athletes would not be paid for competing, but they would have the right to earn their livelihood in any manner they choose.* This would be a simple, realistic, and equitable code.[4]

Excluding the objections of crusty old amateur officials, the

---

4. Bruce Kidd, in one of the most perceptive pieces of sports journalism I have ever read, makes a distinction between professionalism and commercialism in athletics (1970, pp. 257–274). Kidd views professionalism as entailing nothing more than allowing athletes to be paid for competing, thus enabling them to devote full-time to developing their athletic skills. Commercialism, on the other hand, involves the ownership and control of a sport, and this is where abuses arise. Under commercialized athletics, players become the property of owners, and owners in their quest for private profit usually trample on the rights of athletes and sometimes even fans. Unfortunately, in the United States with its private-profit economy, professionalism has always entailed commercialism.

Kidd—and I would agree with him—is in favor of professionalizing sport, but is opposed to commercializing it. This is quite obviously a radical proposal, and even though it's a very sound one, it is not likely to happen in the near future either in Canada where Kidd is a citizen or here in the United States. However, it is not a utopian proposal, for there are many individuals both in Canada and the United States struggling to create a humane society with a non-private-profit economy where this kind of proposal would be readily adopted. Kidd's proposal, as I am sure he would be the first to admit, is not a panacea; but it is an important step in the right direction and will, wherever instituted, contribute significantly to the eventual humanization of sport. This issue points out how the true humanization of sport is dependent on the concomitant humanization of society.

main opposition to this proposal will come from those athletes who are unable, or unwilling, to devote more than a few hours each week to sport. Their complaint will be that they will not have the opportunity to get to the top if they have to compete against athletes who are spending what seems to them an inordinate amount of time training. The athletes who will voice this complaint often refer to themselves as true amateurs, and that being the case, I will only remind them that the main ideal of true amateurism is that the value of sport is supposed to be intrinsic. If they are really the amateurs they like to consider themselves, it will not matter that they can no longer win national or international championships. Most of the benefits—social, physical, and psychological—to be gained from athletics are not dependent on a person's performing in international competition. These individuals will be able to train, or not train, to their hearts' content, and they will have no trouble finding exciting, stimulating competition.

At no time have I based my argument for a revision of the existing amateur code on the grounds that the present code is repeatedly and flagrantly violated. This would have been spurious reasoning, for the worth of a principle in no way depends on whether people obey it. Ideals such as honesty and brotherhood among all men are as valid today as they ever were, even though very few people have ever truly followed them. Neither have I used the argument that Western nations must relax amateur rules so their athletes can keep up with athletes from socialistic or communistic countries. This argument implies that athletes are little more than hired gladiators who perform primarily for the glory of their nation.

The fundamental ideal of any new code of amateurism should declare that track and field is a beautiful, noble activity conducted primarily for the benefit of individual athletes. This is an inspirational, but realistic ideal, worthy of man's highest respect —all other matters pertaining to the code would be of secondary importance. Officials and administrators would check to insure that athletes were not receiving direct payment for competing or using dangerous drugs, but most of their time would be spent working *for* athletes rather than *against* them, as they are forced to do under the existing code.

10

Athletes and the Student Movement

UNIVERSITY OF CALIFORNIA ATHLETES REFUSE TO COMPETE UNTIL THE VIETNAM WAR IS OVER. Seem unlikely? Well, it is, but after events on the Berkeley campus during the spring of 1970, a lot of people, including a worried athletic director and many angry alums, are beginning to wonder just how unlikely.

Despite the escalation in student activism on the Berkeley campus ever since the Free Speech Movement in 1964, Cal athletes had, until recently, remained steadfastly isolated from the student movement. In the past, the athletic department was able to proudly proclaim that none of their boys had ever been involved in student demonstrations. What the athletic department meant was that Cal athletes had never actively supported the student movement; athletes had been involved in demonstrations on a number of occasions when they beat up their fellow students who were peacefully demonstrating.

The Cal athletic department staff has been even more removed from the campus community than the athletes have been. Their offices occupy the entire fourth floor of Eshleman Hall, the student activities building, and their antiseptic sterility provides a startling contrast to the rest of the building. On the walls of the elevator that takes you to their fourth floor offices are scrawled the kind of slogans you would expect to find in a student building at Berkeley—"Free Bobby," "Riot On!" "Judge Hoffman is a Geritol freak." But when you step off the elevator onto the fourth floor, it's like suddenly entering a 1950 movie set. The first thing you see is a line-up of photographs of formidable-looking Golden Bear gridiron greats. Then there are the coaches. With one or two exceptions, they are cut uniformly from the John Wayne mold—clean-cut and square of jaw. Head football coach Ray Willsey, for instance, still believes that nearly everyone on campus is concerned about Cal's chances of making it to the Rose Bowl. And Paul Brechler, the athletic director, is trying hard to stop referring to Cal's black athletes as "colored boys," although he sometimes slips up. Talking to a group of students at the school of education, Brechler responded to a question from a black graduate student about why he seemed so fond of one particular black football player. "I like John because he's always laughing and grinning," Brechler told the startled student, "and that's the kind of colored boy I like."

It was in this atmosphere that I began teaching a course at Cal during the winter of 1970 entitled, "Intercollegiate Athletics and Higher Education: A Socio-Psychological Evaluation." Despite the prominent role intercollegiate athletics plays on nearly every major college campus in the country, a course of this nature had never been offered, either at Berkeley or at any other school. The Cal athletic department was upset with the course from the day it was first announced.

Approximately four hundred students, over one hundred of whom were athletes, enrolled in the course by the second week. During the first lecture, I discussed my involvement in athletics and politics. I told the class I would not be impartial in my own presentations, but would try to foster a rigorous examination of significant issues by opening the class to whomever cared to attend, including members of the athletic department. I invited guest lecturers ranging from Harry Edwards and Dave Meggyesy to conservative spokesman in the athletic world such as Payton Jordon, 1968 U.S. Olympic track and field coach, and Max Rafferty. Rafferty was a highly successful high school football coach many years ago when he first began teaching, and today he regularly gives speeches on the character-building value of athletics (see Chapter 2 for one of Rafferty's speeches). Jordon and Rafferty, along with Cal's football coach Ray Willsey, who said he was too busy recruiting high school football prospects, turned down my invitation to speak to the class. The majority of guest lecturers were liberal/radicals with a humanistic approach to sport. Regrettably, conservative spokesmen were unwilling to come to the class and speak before an audience that might rigorously challenge their ideas.

One of the most significant aspects of the course was that an environment was created in which athletes could begin to examine their role in sport. We discussed the effect their participation in sport had on their personal development and on society. The course was very emotional at times, especially for the athletes, many of whom were beginning to question for the first time their involvement in sport. Racism in athletics was examined throughout the course, and many of the white athletes eventually began to show some understanding of the problems their black teammates encounter.

I realized many athletes had changed their attitudes toward their own involvement in sport and the role of athletics within the university by the time the course ended. But I did not know if these new attitudes would ever be reflected in their behavior. I was still pondering the impact of the course when President Nixon announced he had sent U.S. troops into Cambodia.

Within a few days, the campus went topsy-turvy in a fury of anti-war activity, and on May 11, students, employees, and faculty members jammed into mammoth Harmon Gymnasium for a mass rally. It was the third mass meeting on campus in as many days, but over 10,000 people—the largest crowd ever to fill the gym—turned out. The bleachers were packed tightly and people were sitting on the basketball court, in the press box, and standing in the aisles. Hundreds of people were outside, unable to get in because of the overflow crowd. The meeting began with speeches by Tom Hayden and Jon Turner, a member of the campus Black Student Union. It then settled down to a discussion and finally a vote on the course of action the university community should take in response to the national and international turmoil created by the Nixon decision.

During the rally three Cal athletes wearing their letterman jackets were seated near me in the balcony of the gym. When they got up and walked out after the third or fourth speech, I heard the person next to me say, "Well, I guess it's time for practice. What's wrong with those guys? Doesn't anything affect them?" His friend whispered to him to be quiet, obviously fearing the athletes might come over and beat up on them.

I imagine that these sentiments were echoed throughout the crowd, since well over one hundred other Cal athletes were leaving the rally at about the same time. But people should have stopped to notice the change in the athletes' appearance. Despite the objection of the athletic director and some coaches, many of those leaving the meeting had long hair and beards or mustaches and were wearing strike buttons and black armbands. Nor were they going to practice; rather, they were on their way to a general meeting of all athletes to discuss what action they, as a group, could take against the government's Southeast Asian policy. This was one day when athletic business did not take place as usual.

This meeting was first suggested by Randy Smyth, a sports columnist for the school newspaper, *The Daily Californian*. Randy, an All-American football player in junior college and later a University of California school record-holder in track and field, is a graduate student and was an unofficial teaching assistant for the course I had taught. He was regularly involved in radical activities on campus, and his long hair and political activism constantly had him in trouble with his coaches while he was competing. Most coaches now refuse to talk to him.

From his extensive contact with Cal athletes, Randy felt they were ready to take some kind of stand against the war if they could just be gathered together in a group. He arranged a preliminary meeting between myself, the *Daily Californian* sports editor Lewis Leader, and five or six Cal athletes who he knew were strongly opposed to the war. Given the climate on campuses throughout the country, we all agreed that it was the ideal time to attempt to get Cal athletes to take the first steps that would lead to involvement in the student movement.

The meeting was announced in the sports pages of the school paper, and the sports editor helped to stimulate interest by running interviews with prominent Cal athletes who were angered and upset by the Cambodian invasion. Much to everyone's amazement, including those of us who organized the meeting, over 150 athletes, along with a worried athletic director and a few coaches, showed up. Mike Fletcher, captain of the crew team, and John Sanford, a black football player, ran the meeting. They both were openly opposed to the Cambodian invasion and the war, and gave short talks in which they stressed the need for athletes to take a united stand. Mike Mohler, a former football player, spoke about the polarization between athletes and the general student body and urged the athletes to unite with their fellow students in opposition to the war.

Once it became clear that the overwhelming majority of athletes present was opposed to the war, the meeting turned to a discussion of how they could best express their dissent. They agreed with the campus sentiment that "business should not go on as usual," but were divided on the question of whether or not to continue practicing and competing. Those opposed to competing felt that since athletics was the most visible part of the university, the only way they could show that business was not as usual with them was by refusing to compete and devoting the time normally spent on athletics to anti-war activities. They also felt that their willingness to give up athletics temporarily would emphasize the seriousness of their commitment. Others argued that they should capitalize on their visibility by continuing to compete, but making their position known by wearing symbols of protest on their uniforms. There were other suggestions that the group sign petitions and issue a public statement in opposition to the war. Paul Brechler, the athletic director, also spoke out, but from a different viewpoint. "I've been in a couple of wars," he said, "and nobody likes war, but I wouldn't want to see you mix up college athletics with the war."

The question of whether or not to compete was a difficult one for the whole group to handle, since not all sports were currently involved in competition. For instance, the basketball players, whose season was over, felt they had no right to vote on whether or not the track athletes should compete for the rest of their season. The athletes, therefore, broke up into groups according to their sport and debated what action to take as a team. After about one half-hour of debate, the meeting reconvened. Steve Sawin, a student who had never before been involved in any form of protest activity, served as the spokesman for the football team. Sawin told the group that the football team had decided to skip the rest of spring practice and involve themselves in some type of antiwar activity. He also added that the football players would attempt to protect any striking athlete against possible reprisals. The wrestling team voted to boycott the National AAU wrestling championships, and all other teams (except the baseball team) issued statements condemning the war and asking for withdrawal of all U.S. troops from Southeast Asia. The track and field and tennis teams, which were competing in Los Angeles over the weekend, indicated they would wear black armbands, clenched-fist patches, and other symbols of protest while competing.

PAUL BRECHLER, athletic director at the University of California, Berkeley (*Photo courtesy Micki Scott*).

Paul Brechler, who admits he would not have taken the athletic director's job a few years ago if he had known what it was going to be like at Cal, talked with me after the meeting. "I just don't know what is going on. If this issue is settled, there will just be another one in the fall." I asked him how he felt about the possibility of Cal athletes wearing symbols of protest while competing. "We have a hundred year old tradition of what is the standard Cal uniform," he told me, "and I'd be personally embarrassed if the boys wore black armbands or black legbands or anything like that. I can't see what it will accomplish. The next thing you know, they'll want to wear shirts saying 'Blake's Bakery.'" He did emphasize that athletes have the right to speak out as individuals, but that their protest should in no way involve sports.

Television crews, photographers, and sports writers crowded into a small conference room in the athletic department the following afternoon to attend a press conference called by the athletes. Ray Willsey, the head football coach, sat at a table flanked by two football players and three other prominent Cal athletes. Willsey was there in his capacity as assistant athletic director, since Brechler had left Berkeley that morning to attend a meeting in Los Angeles.

The football players announced that they had decided to resume practicing after having a number of meetings with Coach Willsey since the previous afternoon. Willsey did not directly threaten the football players at these meetings. He stressed the importance of spring practice and then simply asked them to individually explain to the coaching staff their reasons for wanting to skip the final five days of spring ball. Regrettably—though quite understandably—most of the football players were not able to tell Coach Willsey that they were more concerned about the war than about spring football practice. They well knew what the eventual consequences would be with regard to their football careers under Willsey if they ever made such a statement.

But the football players, along with the athletes from all the other Cal teams, did issue the following statement signed by the United Athletes of the University of California:

We, the overwhelming majority of California athletes, find that we can no longer live in the so-called "apolitical atmosphere" which has permeated the athletic community. We find it necessary now to voice our opposition to President Nixon's oppressive policies at home and abroad. We condemn United States activity in Southeast Asia and call for a unilateral withdrawal of all United States forces in Southeast Asia. Furthermore, we call for a reconstitution of American universities as centers against the war.

Whatever fire the football players had lost was made up for by the remarks of Bob McLennan, captain of the track and field team, and Mike Mullan of the tennis team. The bearded McLennan, who was active in student government, told the assembled press that the Nixon-ordered invasion of Cambodia was a betrayal of the trust the American people had placed in the President. He spoke in support of efforts being made to reconstitute the university as a center for anti-war activities and emphasized, "The university will not return to normal until the war is ended." Mullan, speaking for the tennis team, condemned "the genocidal war in Southeast Asia" and said that the tennis players would wear shirts with anti-war slogans in place of their regular uniforms in a match scheduled for that weekend in Los Angeles.

This outburst at Cal has calmed down, but things have not returned to normal. They probably never will. Berkeley athletes had struck another blow at the stereotype of the dumb, crewcut, mumbling jock. Their acts were not isolated, but were part of the simmering revolt that increasingly characterizes college athletics throughout the country. Scores of college athletes have joined the student movement, not as fellow travelers temporarily caught up in the emotional momentum of anti-war activity, but as committed strugglers alongside their fellow students.

At the 1970 Heptagonal Track and Field Championships, the captains and representatives of the eight Ivy League schools in the ten-school Heptagonal Games Association issued such a strong political statement shortly before the meet was to begin that the Army and Navy teams withdrew, only moments before the first event. The statement not only condemned the war, but spoke out against "the repression of the Black Panther Party and people of radical disposition in general." They further mentioned

Bob McLennan, captain of the 1970 University of California NCAA Championship track team: "We, the overwhelming majority of California athletes, find that we can no longer live in the so-called 'apolitical atmosphere' which has permeated the athletic community. We find it necessary now to voice our opposition to President Nixon's oppressive policies at home and abroad" (*Photo courtesy Micki Scott*).

that ". . . as athletes and track men, we understand that our sport is not and must never become a hideout from our basic responsibilities as human beings." This statement was issued by those athletes who chose to compete, but 45 other top Ivy League track athletes, including Harvard's star miler Royce Shaw, registered their protest by boycotting the meet entirely.

At Columbia, where only a year or two before athletes under the direction of the crew coach had organized themselves into right-wing vigilante groups and beat up on their fellow students during campus demonstrations, eighty-five football players endorsed a petition supporting a nationwide student strike; and baseball, track, tennis, and golf athletes voted to cancel their competition. And at Stanford University, Mal Snider, a former Stanford All-American football player, was among those students who staged a sit-in at the campus ROTC building.

Athletic protests during the spring of 1970 even reached into the heartland of America. At the University of Kansas, Sam Goldberg, the number three ranked college decathlon man in the country, was kicked off the team and had his scholarship cancelled for what he feels were political reasons. Goldberg had announced he planned to make some form of peaceful protest at the NCAA Track and Field Championships in order to protest the killing of students at Kent State and Jackson State. The athletic department claimed he violated a number of their regulations and was disruptive to team morale (New York *Times,* June 23, 1970, p. 50).

But while scores of athletes all over the country were joining the student movement, NCAA officials and executives were rushing to join Spiro Agnew's silent majority movement. Walter Byers, executive director of the NCAA, announced that the NCAA, working in conjunction with the Defense Department, was sending eight college athletic stars to Vietnam and the Far East to help troop morale and ". . . give GIs an insight into and a favorable image of campus life" (NCAA *News,* June 1970, p. 1). Five of the eight athletes selected were from southern colleges, and, almost needless to say, none of those sent had been involved in any anti-war activities. But the NCAA's attempt to portray college athletes as being patriotic supporters of the government's Southeast Asian policies was not entirely successful. During the height of the protests after the Cambodian invasion, a spokesman for the Nixon administration commented, "Once we heard that the athletes and pom-pom girls had joined the demonstrations, we knew we were in trouble."

PART II

SCIENCE AND SPORT

We are a civilization committed to the quest for continually improved means to carelessly examined ends.

Robert Merton (1964)

11

The Sport Psychologist
—Friend or Foe?

This is an edited version of a talk I gave to the North American Society for the Psychology of Sport and Physical Activity in Seattle during the spring of 1970. I discuss contemporary conditions in intercollegiate athletics and examine the social responsibility of the sport psychologist, including the implicit value assumptions these men often make. I am especially critical of those sport psychologists who adopt the methods and values of industrial psychologists in their work with high school and college athletes and coaches. Sport psychology, like any other branch of the social sciences, will not automatically work for the benefit of man. Whether or not the sport psychologist is a friend or foe of those working to build a humanistic approach to sport is entirely dependent on the value orientation of the individual sport psychologist.

I especially want to thank Dr. Bryant Cratty, the President of the North American Society for the Psychology of Sport and Physical Activity, for inviting me to talk here today. At a time when an ever increasing number of young people are beginning not only to question but also to totally reject many societal activities—and I for one happen to believe they have good reason for their questioning and rejecting even though I may not personally agree with the wisdom of all their actions—it was most heartening for me to receive this invitation. I was heartened by Dr. Cratty's invitation for it indicated to me a willingness on his part, and on the part of this society, to squarely face up to the very real and urgent problems confronting the sports world.

I must admit that when I first received the invitation I had no idea who Jack Cratty was, and I momentarily thought he might have invited me in the same spirit the powers that be in the Pentagon might have invited C. Wright Mills to speak to them. To my knowledge, Mills was never invited by the war lords, but they did invite Paul Goodman. Goodman promptly accepted their invitation, and just as promptly turned his honorarium over to the war resistance movement!

I've been involved in sports for eighteen years. In high school I participated primarily in boxing, football, and track. I attended Stanford University on a track scholarship and concentrated on this sport in college. In the last few years, I've been active as a coach, sports writer, and most recently as a teacher at the University of California at Berkeley, examining the role of intercollegiate athletics in higher education. I came here today to talk with you, not at you, and I hope this is the spirit in which you will take my remarks. I'll try to share my experiences and observations with you, and I hope you will do the same with me.

There are three issues that I would like you to keep in mind throughout my talk. The first is the value orientation of sport psychology. With regard to this issue, I'd like to read a brief statement from Robert Merton's introduction to Jacques Ellul's book, *The Technological Society*. "We are a civilization committed to the quest for continually improved means to carelessly examined ends" (1964, p. vi). Merton's statement will become particularly relevant later on in my talk, for as I will point out, we must begin to examine critically the ends to which our efforts as sport psychologists are being used.

The second point I'd like you to keep in mind is whom is the sport psychologist to be the agent of. This issue, along with the question of the value orientation of sport psychology, becomes especially significant when we look at the work of Drs. Ogilvie and Tutko, particularly their book, *Problem Athletes and How to*

Handle Them. Thomas S. Szasz, a psychiatrist with whose work many of you are familiar, speaks directly to the question of whom the psychologist is to be the agent of in one of his many books, *The Ethics of Psychoanalysis* (1965, p. 21):

> By the time Freud became a physician, two roles had been established for the psychiatrist. They are still widely accepted. One is the role of society's agent; the state-hospital psychiatrist, while appearing to minister to the patient, actually protects society from the patient. The other is the role of everyone's agent and of no one's; an arbiter of the conflicts between patient and family, patient and employer, and so forth, such a psychiatrist's allegiance is to whomever pays him. Freud refused to play either of these roles. Instead he created a new one—agent of the patient. In my opinion, this is his greatest contribution to psychiatry.

To bring Szasz's statement into the sports world, I only need to point out that an act which is in the best interest of a football coach is not necessarily in the best interest of a football player, and the sport psychologist cannot always be the agent of both these individuals. I'll give you a specific example of what I mean. Not too many years ago there was a football coach who hired a psychologist to administer intelligence tests to all prospective players each year at the opening of training camp. Those players who scored at both extremes of the test were usually dismissed from the team by the coach. The low scorers were dismissed on the grounds that they wouldn't be able to learn the complicated techniques of modern football, and the high scorers on the grounds that they often prove difficult to coach! This is a clear-cut case of a psychologist being hired by a coach to work in the coach's best interest regardless of the consequences for the players. This psychologist was working as the agent of the coach, not the athletes. Perhaps you can better understand what I'm saying if you consider what the coach's reaction would have been if the athletes hired a psychologist to test his fitness to coach!

Though I gave a rather extreme example, I'm sure all of you can think of many cases where there are real conflicts of interest between the coach and athlete. This is especially true in our colleges and universities where, often times, authoritarian coaches treat college students as if they were professional athletes. Ideally, it is of course possible for the sport psychologist to be both agent of the coach and the athlete, but I'm afraid this is the exception rather than the rule—at least with respect to college athletics in the United States.

The third and last point I'd like you to keep in mind throughout my talk is the reality behind the image of the sports world—an image of the sports world that has been created by the multi-million dollar American sports industry. As Leonard Shecter points out in his excellent book, *The Jocks,* all too many sports writers have been little more than public relations men for college and professional teams. For those of you who want to get a realistic understanding of conditions in the American sports world today, I strongly suggest you tune in to the new breed of sports writer developing in the country. We, as scholars, can learn much from the journalistic writings of men like Pete Axthelm, the sports editor of *Newsweek;* Bob Lipsyte, a New York *Times* sports columnist; Sandy Padwe of the Philadelphia *Inquirer;* Stan Isaacs of *Newsday;* and Dave Burgin, the executive sports editor of the San Francisco *Examiner.* These men, and other sports writers like them throughout the country, are accurately and honestly writing about the contemporary sports scene.[1] In my opinion, familiarity with the work of these men is as indispensable to us as knowledge of proper research methodology.

As American sport psychologists, we are an integral part of American society; and we must always remember this even if we, at times, quite understandably, might like to forget it. It would be both foolhardy and socially irresponsible for us to carry on as if

1. The following is a list of some other sports writers you can count on for an accurate and honest description of contemporary developments in the sports world. This list is by no means inclusive. Larry Merchant, New York *Post;* George Kiseda, Philadelphia *Bulletin;* Neil Amdur, *New York Times;* Phil Finch, San Francisco *Examiner;* Joe Henderson, *The Runner's World;* Dave Wolfe, a free-lancer; Ira Berkow of NEA; and Wells Twombly of the San Francisco *Examiner.* A most encouraging sign in recent years has been the perceptive sports writing appearing in college newspapers around the country. The American sports world will be a much better place if individuals like Lewis Leader and Brent Tempest, recent sports editors of the *Daily Californian* at the University of California, and Jim Cohen, recent sports editor of the school paper at the University of Wisconsin, continue on as professional sports writers after college graduation.

our work existed in a vacuum. I think we're all aware, or at least we should be, that a lot of weird and frightening things have been happening in the last few months. The revolutionary rhetoric of some radicals has become a reality, and we've seen bombings in nearly every major American city. We see our government, as Martin Luther King so aptly pointed out, using might and force to get its own way overseas while condemning those who use these same tactics here at home. We have ecological problems that con- servatives, liberals, radicals, everyone can recognize, even members of those industries that are daily destroying the ecology. In the opinion of many, we are beginning to see a rise of political repres- sion unparalleled since the days of Joe McCarthy. The chief target of this political repression to date has been the Black Panther Party. The government seems set on destroying the Panthers using means ranging from legal procedures to early morning raids such as the recent one in Chicago where police shot to death Fred Hampton, the Illinois Party leader, while he lay unarmed in his bed. The question at issue here is not whether we agree or disagree with the philosophy and tactics of the Black Panther Party. The real issue is whether or not there is to be liberty and justice for all, or only for those groups and individuals who pose no real threat to the existing order.

I'm sure you're all aware of the recent Chicago 8 trial, and however you may feel about that trial, I think we all can agree that there is something drastically wrong when there can be such a mockery of justice in American society. The constitutionality of the law under which the eight men were indicted should be challenged since it could be used effectively to inhibit any political movement that earns the disfavor of the government. I'm still pondering the wisdom of some of the behavior of the Chicago 8 defendants; but I am shocked and dismayed by the behavior of Judge Julius Hoff- man, especially his treatment of a black man, Bobby Seale, who demanded nothing more than the right to defend himself in the ab- sence of an attorney of his own choice.

We, as sports psychologists, must be aware of the polarization and repression occurring in society, for the sports world has not, and cannot be expected to, remain aloof from these occurrences. In the sports world, as in society at large, individuals representing an authoritarian, anti-life force are lining up in opposition to those representing a creative, humanistic life force. The conflicts between these two groups do not stem from a simple lack of communication or misunderstanding as some would have us believe. These two positions represent fundamentally opposed views of life.[2] When we enter the sports world to do our research and applied work, we have to make the choice of which of these two forces we are going to support. If we are going to work for whoever will pay us, including racist, authoritarian coaches, and athletic administrators, we must recognize to which side we are giving our support.

The racism extant in sport is one of the most critical problems that we must begin to come to grips with. Dr. John Loy, an officer of this society, has written an excellent paper on the problem of segregation in sport. It is a well-researched paper and makes many important points. But still, we only have to look around this room, and we can recognize, or at least we should recognize, that people could very easily talk about institutionalized racism in academic professions, including this society. While I'm sure that most of you have not consciously excluded blacks from this society, the simple fact is that there is only one black person here today. I cannot help but believe that after this society becomes more fully integrated, we will be in a better position to examine critically the problem of racism in sport. Additionally, I think it is time we begin to recognize that, when as many as 30%–40% of the athletes with whom we are working are black, black social scientists can make meaningful contributions that perhaps we, from a white perspective, cannot.

I would also like to make one additional suggestion along this same line. As the Women's Liberation people would say, it is time we become cognizant of our male chauvinism and begin to do something about it. Not only is this society made up almost entirely of males, but nearly all our research is directed to assisting male athletes. Sexism, no less than racism, is a problem which any group that hopes to make meaningful contributions to society must eliminate.

2. For those of you who are hesitant to agree with this statement, I suggest you read Max Rafferty's speech, Chapter 2.

ATHLETICS AND HIGHER EDUCATION

Before addressing myself to the question of the value orientation of sports psychology and who the sports psychologist is to be the agent of, I want to spend a short time discussing contemporary conditions in college athletics. The University of California at Berkeley has served as a barometer for the student movement ever since the Free Speech Movement in 1964, and I believe that it will perform the same function for what I would call the athletic movement. As many of you know, I recently taught a course at Berkeley entitled Intercollegiate Athletics and Higher Education: A Socio-Psychological Evaluation. To my knowledge, a course of this nature had never been taught in the history of American higher education. I'd like to share with you a few of the many insights I gained from the guest lecturers and students, many of whom were athletes, who participated in the course.

One of the most significant things about the course was the response to it, both at Berkeley and throughout the United States. Approximately 400 students, including over 100 varsity athletes, enrolled in the course. Guest lecturers flew in from all over the country at their own expense. Harry Edwards, who normally commands a guest lecturer fee of $1,000 to $1,500, came in at his own expense. Dave Meggyesy, a professional football player for the St. Louis Cardinals, flew in from St. Louis at his own expense. Curt Canning, captain of the Harvard crew team that went to the Mexico City Olympics and supported the Olympic Project for Human Rights, left medical school at the University of Utah for four days and flew to Berkeley at his own expense in order to participate in the course. *Newsweek* magazine sent their sports editor, Pete Axthelm, out from New York so that he could participate in a panel discussion on the role of the news media in covering college athletics. Some of these individuals and the many other guest lecturers who participated in the course at their own expense may have done so partly because of a personal friendship with me, but I believe their primary reason was their concern with contemporary conditions in the sports world, especially college athletics. Many of them felt, and I believe quite correctly, that if courses like this could spring up on college campuses throughout the country, there would be a chance for the desperately needed changes in intercollegiate athletics to come about in a peaceful, constructive manner.

I learned much about some of the problems in intercollegiate athletics from the athletes enrolled in the course. One of the most salient problems that was brought to my attention is that of the widespread drug usage among college athletes. About four weeks ago, the Cal team physician made a presentation at a national medical conference in San Francisco where he said that a very small percentage of Cal football players have used amphetamines and other speed drugs while participating in intercollegiate athletics. He emphasized that there was no real problem, for the usage was restricted to a relatively few athletes, and even with them it was on an experimental basis. However, a football player taking the course, Mike Mohler, did a paper on drug usage among Cal football players. He talked to every player on the team and found that over 48% of them used amphetamines and other speed drugs while playing football. His report also showed that 28% of the football players were using, or had used, anabolic steroids. In talking with Mike about his study, he mentioned to me that he felt the use of these drugs was even more common at other West Coast, big-time football schools than at Berkeley.

The same coaches who will dismiss an athlete from the team for getting drunk or blowing a little grass are frequently making speed drugs and steroids—drugs far more dangerous in almost any medical doctor's evaluation—available to their athletes or turning their heads while athletes use them. From my own experience as an athlete and coach in track and field, I know that drug usage has increased significantly in this sport over the past few years. One of the most famous United States gold medal winners at the Mexico City Olympics, a man who was honored as the ideal amateur athlete, carries enough drugs around with him to open up a drug store!

This whole area of drug usage is one that we should begin to examine. One of the fundamental questions we may want to ask is just what is happening to athletics and athletes when participants are resorting to these kinds of dangerous and sometimes lethal artificial aids to help their sports performance.

Another problem that I learned about through the course was that of the lack of communication between athletes and coaches. Some of the football players in the course got together and gave a presentation to the class in the form of a panel discussion on what it is like being an athlete on the Berkeley campus. The most interesting part of the discussion was the presentation of the three black athletes who participated. I say it was the most interesting because they were the only panelists who talked about their personal experiences as athletes. The other members of the panel tried to give a so-called scholarly presentation giving statistics and abstract views of the football experience, and totally avoided talking about their personal involvement in the game. This, of course, would have been their strong point since anyone could have distributed the questionnaires, collected the data, and figured the statistics that they did, but only these particular individuals could speak about their unique experiences as football players.

The black panelists, while speaking from their own point of view, also did some research. They spoke to about eighteen black former football players at Cal and discovered that everyone of them, to a man, was bitter about his athletic experiences. Approximately 90% of them felt there was rampant racism within the Cal athletic department, and not one among them was happy with what was going on in the department at the time they attended Cal. But if you talk to the coaches, they will say there were, and are, no real problems. The problems of course exist, but they are simply being suppressed, and this is the reason they can't understand why every once in awhile there is a big explosion. A coach will say, perhaps in good faith, "We haven't had problems here for four years. Why the explosion all of a sudden? I can't understand it." Well, the reason there is an explosion is because there is no real communication between the coaching staff and the athletes, and finally the problems build up to a point where some kind of action must be taken.

This problem of lack of communication, particularly as it exists between coaches and black athletes, is growing more subtle as coaches are beginning to change. In the past there were coaches and athletic directors, like the athletic director at the University of Texas at El Paso, who simply said to a national sports reporter, "We treat our nigger athletes good." These kinds of overt racist statements and acts rarely occur anymore. The problems arise, however, when coaches who do not communicate with black athletes have to make the judgmental decisions that coaches frequently must make. Often when the coach's decision goes against them, the black athletes will assume, and many times justifiably so, that the decision made was a racist one whether or not it actually was. And these problems will continue to arise until coaches begin to actively demonstrate that they are men of good will and open real channels of communication through which black and white athletes can redress their grievances. The feeble attempt by some athletic departments to "pacify" the black athletes by hiring black assistant coaches has only intensified, in many cases, the blacks' suspicion of white racism by the type of Negroes often being hired for these positions.

An example of the lack of communication that exists between athletes and coaches at a school like Berkeley was brought up during the panel discussion by Cal football players. At the beginning of the football season last year, the head coach said to the team, "Anyone who has any problems should come and talk to me and we'll straighten it out." Apparently not one person went to the coach during the entire season. Yet when a questionnaire was distributed to the players at the conclusion of the season, well over 50% of them said they had real problems that they wished they could have discussed with the coach. From past experience, the players felt that the coach was not really interested in listening to their problems, and would just dismiss anyone who had problems as someone who "didn't have what it takes to play football."

A coach who sincerely wants to begin communicating with his athletes has to do more than simply invite them to come to his office with their grievances. Athletes are often suspicious of coaches who extend this kind of invitation, and their suspicion is not entirely unfounded. In the past, many coaches who claimed they wanted to communicate with their athletes wound up labeling any athlete who came forth with grievances a troublemaker. A coach who wants to avoid major disruptions must be willing to involve himself in serious discussions with his athletes and take action on their legitimate grievances.

There are many coaches who, though having a genuine concern for the athletes they work with, are finding it difficult to open up and begin honestly communicating with them. These coaches feel that they will lose their authority and the athletes' respect if they begin behaving in a democratic manner. We should point out to these men that behaving in a democratic manner does not necessarily lead to a breakdown of discipline or loss of respect.

However, I would be remiss if I didn't point out that many athletes will often interpret democratic behavior or kindness on the part of a coach as a sign of weakness. Because of the rampant authoritarianism that permeates the administrative and coaching ranks of the American sports world, athletes who themselves are not authoritarian are usually quickly filtered out of sport at a very young age. This filtering process begins as early as Little League Baseball, Pop Warner Football, and age group swimming where the "correct" attitude is often as important as athletic skill.

Mindless obedience seems to be the most essential ingredient for success in many American sports. In fact, when coaches talk of discipline—a quality I'm sure we all would agree is necessary for success in athletics—they really are talking about obedience. To most American coaches, an obedient athlete is a disciplined athlete, even though he may not have the least bit of self-discipline. Non-authoritarian or "free-spirited" athletes find it difficult to stomach American style athletics; and if they choose to continue competing rather than quit, these individuals are usually branded "uncoachables" or "troublemakers." Not surprisingly, given the nature of the American sports scene, a very large percentage of American athletes are quite authoritarian, and these athletes will usually only respect an authoritarian, "hard-liner" coach. A coach who gets a negative feedback every time be behaves in a non-authoritarian manner with the athletes he coaches is not likely to change his behavior. Consequently, when attempting to attenuate authoritarianism in sport, we must be aware that athletes are sometimes just as authoritarian as coaches and administrators.

There are coaches such as Jim Klein, the track coach at Westmont College in Santa Barbara, California, Harry Parker, the Har-

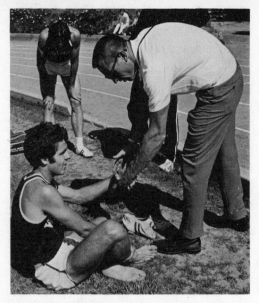

JIM KLEIN, head track coach at Westmont College in Santa Barbara, California. Klein was an outstanding decathlon performer as an athlete, and now, as a coach, he is making an honest and committed effort to adjust to contemporary conditions in the athletic world. He is one of the most successful young track coaches in America today.

HARRY PARKER, head crew coach at Harvard and one of America's most successful coaches. One of Parker's greatest strengths is his openness and willingness to learn from the athletes he coaches. Unlike most coaches, Parker treats athletes with dignity and respect. Not surprisingly, Parker is one of the relatively few coaches who have the unqualified respect of the athletes they coached (*Jet Photographers, Courtesy of Harvard University Athletic Department*).

vard crew coach, and Dan Milman, the gymnastics coach at Stanford, who have struggled hard to change themselves so that they could relate to the athletes they coach in a humane, dignified manner. It is these kinds of coaches that, in my opinion, deserve our support and encouragement. We should use our expertise as sport psychologists to examine and record the struggle of these men and the athletes they coach. They have successfully made the transition from an authoritarian style of coaching to a more humane one, and there is much to be learned from understanding the dynamics of this change.

One of the most shocking things I learned from the athletes enrolled in the course was the degree of mistrust and outright hostility that often exist between black and white athletes. At this point, let me mention that this situation is not unique to Cal; it exists on nearly every high school, college, and professional team in the country. Blacks, usually justifiably so, are convinced that their white teammates receive favored treatment from the coaches, whereas the white athletes often believe that the blacks are allowed to get away with behavior that the coaches would not tolerate from them. The white players feel that the coaches are afraid to discipline the blacks for fear of a boycott or some kind of demonstration. The mistrust and hostility between black and white athletes exist to such a degree that there is almost no meaningful communication between these two groups. Once they leave the playing field, the black and white athletes go their separate ways. And whenever a conflict arises between the black athletes and the athletic department, regardless of the reasons for the conflict, the white athletes invariably align themselves on the side of the coaches and athletic department.

Despite the plethora of team meetings coaches hold during a season, they almost never devote even one of these meetings to the question of racial relations on the squad. The St. Louis Cardinals professional football team is a good example of this. The rampant racism that existed on the Cardinals was first exposed by Jack Olsen in 1968 in his fine series of articles entitled, "The Black Athlete: A Shameful Story." The racist situation that Olsen exposed existed for over five years, but during that period, the Cardinals did not have one team meeting to discuss the situation even though the players and coaches were all well aware of what was going on. The first team meeting the coaches had to discuss the problem was not called until immediately after they received an advance copy of Olsen's article a few days before it was scheduled to appear in *Sports Illustrated*. And that meeting—a meeting which ended with head coach Charley Winner suggesting all the players go out and drink a few beers at the local tavern previously reserved for only white players—was the only meeting the Cardinals held to discuss the racism on the team. Even during this meeting, the coaches and most of the white players refused to recognize there were any real problems. They took the position that *Sports Illustrated* had greatly exaggerated the situation in order to sell magazines!

Before moving on to a discussion of the work of Drs. Ogilvie and Tutko, I'd like to share a final bit of information I learned through teaching the course. During the last class session, I distributed a questionnaire to all those students present. I believe the data gathered from this questionnaire has relevance beyond saying something about the 400 students enrolled in the course. As I mentioned earlier, Berkeley students have served as a barometer for the student movement, and I believe they will perform this same function for the athletic movement. The first question I asked was, "Should intercollegiate athletics be abolished?" Approximately 99% of both the athletes and non-athletes responding to this question said "no." Those few individuals who responded with a "yes," qualified their response by saying, "Yes, as they presently exist." I was particularly pleased with the response to this question, for I was a little worried that some of the students might have concluded that the only solution was to abolish intercollegiate athletics, since I and the majority of the guest lecturers had been so critical of most existing athletic programs. (It should be recognized, of course, that for the most part the non-athletes enrolled in the course were individuals quite interested in athletics. I'm sure that in a random sampling of the non-athlete student population at Berkeley, there would be a significant percentage who would favor abolishing intercollegiate athletics.)

The other question I asked that has relevance for us was, "Are major changes needed in intercollegiate athletics?" Approximately 84% of the varsity athletes in the course responded with a "yes" to this question as did 97% of the non-athletes in the course. When the overwhelming majority of athletes feel major changes are needed and the athletic department is resistant to instituting any significant changes, it is not hard to see why the Cal athletic program has been plagued with disruptions, boycotts, and other disturbances. But whether it be at Cal or other institutions, the blame for these disturbances should not be borne solely by the coaches, for it is primarily athletic directors and university administrators who are in charge of making policy. Additionally, it is particularly sad to see the lack of leadership exhibited by the NCAA in these matters.

THE SPORT PSYCHOLOGIST IN ACTION

In the American athletic world, Drs. Bruce Ogilvie and Thomas Tutko are unquestionably the two most well known sport psychologists. For better or worse, athletes, coaches, and athletic administrators throughout the country are forming their impression of what sport psychology is all about on the basis of the work of these two men.

Ogilvie and Tutko's book, *Problem Athletes and How to Handle Them,* is very popular with coaches and equally unpopular with athletes. I believe their approach to sport psychology is captured quite accurately by the title of their book. The phrase "how to handle them" certainly does not exhibit the sensitivity one might expect from psychologists genuinely interested in helping human beings. The book is a cookbook approach to sport psychology that was written with the purpose—as revealed in the title—of enabling coaches to "handle" what they deem to be problem athletes.

For those of you who are unfamiliar with Ogilvie and Tutko's book, I'd like to read some comments from an advertisement for the book that appeared in a catalogue put out by *Track and Field News.* The advertisement will give you some idea of how their book is being used in the sports world. The headlines of the ad read as follows: "NO NEED TO CALL IN THE WITCH DOCTOR FOR YOUR PSYCHED-OUT ATHLETES AND UNDERACHIEVERS. READ *PROBLEM ATHLETES AND HOW TO HANDLE THEM.*" The ad went on to say, "Motivation research involving over 2000 amateur and professional athletes has identified at least seven common types of problem athletes—The Athlete Who Resists Coaching, The Con Man, The Psyched-Out Athlete, The Athlete With Success Phobia, The Injury-Prone Athlete,

The Withdrawn Athlete, and the Depression-Prone Athlete. Procedures for handling these problem athletes, to help them reach their potential, are outlined by the authors. Suggested action is specific and detailed, and is supported by case histories."

Drs. Ogilvie and Tutko have recently expanded their psychological services within the sports world. One of the things they are doing at the present time is sending out psychological tests to coaches who request them. The coach has whatever athlete he wants to take the test, and it is then returned to Ogilvie and Tutko. For a fee of $3.00 per college athlete ($1.50 per high school athlete) they provide the coach with a psychological analysis of the athlete. According to one coach they work with, "These tests give us information so we can know the right buttons to push in order to get maximum performance from our boys."

Now that we have some understanding of the nature of Ogilvie and Tutko's work, I'd like to examine it from the perspective of the three points I asked you to keep in mind during my talk: (1) whom is the sport psychologist to be the agent of, (2) the value orientation of sport psychology, and (3) the reality behind the image of the sports world.

First let's look at Ogilvie and Tutko's work from the perspective of whom they are the agent of. In their work in high school, college, and professional athletics, they are invariably hired by coaches, athletic directors, or professional team owners. They are paid by these men, and, if they did not work in the best interest of these men, their services would not be utilized.

In many ways, their situation is analogous to that of the industrial psychologist who is hired by management to get workers to perform more profitably. The industrial psychologist who works for management may improve conditions for the workers, but this is incidental to his main job which is to increase the profits of the business. Similarly, Ogilvie and Tutko may occasionally help athletes, but this is incidental to their prime task, which is to help coaches have winning teams. The title of their book indicates quite clearly whom they have chosen to become the agent of; just as if I wrote a book entitled *Problem Coaches and How to Handle Them* would indicate whom I had chosen to become the agent of. Some coaches undoubtedly would profit from such a book, but, once again, this would be incidental to the main purpose of the book, which would have been to help athletes. Likewise, if athletes paid me to administer psychological tests to a coach and provide them with a psychological analysis of the coach, I would be working as an agent of the athletes, and it would verge on Machiavellism if I also claimed to be working in the best interest of the coach.

It should be quite clear that Ogilvie and Tutko work as the agent of the coach and not the athlete. They themselves put this matter to rest, for in the introduction to *Problem Athletes and How to Handle Them* they admit, "This handbook is presented with the *coaches' needs* as our primary concern" (1966, p. 11).

The fact that Ogilvie and Tutko work as the agent of the coach is neither cause for commendation nor condemnation. This knowledge alone reveals nothing significant about the nature of their work. However, recognition of this fact coupled with knowledge of the reality of the American sports world does tell us something about their work—something quite significant, as I believe we'll see in a moment.

As I pointed out earlier, Ogilvie and Tutko are presently running a mail order psychological testing service where, for three dollars, they provide a psychological analysis of any athlete who takes their test. Coaches throughout the country are beginning to require athletes to take this test, and, to date, Ogilvie and Tutko have cooperated with any coach who chose to utilize their service. Now, even though some of us may not want to admit it, I'm sure we all recognize there are quite a few coaches around who are rather unpleasant characters. I can't help but think of one of my college coaches who told me about the good feeling I was suppose to get whenever I beat a "nigger," or the former Maryland football coach who openly admits he kicked players during practice, or the Wyoming football coach who last fall dismissed over a dozen black players from the team simply because they wore black armbands as a protest gesture over having to play against Brigham Young.

Now these are not isolated incidents. In fact, quite ironically, it was Drs. Ogilvie and Tutko themselves who told me that after extensively testing coaches throughout the country, they found them to be one of the, if not *the,* most authoritarian group of individuals in our society. Also, Ogilvie and Tutko admit that coaches are not very sensitive to dependency needs in others (1966, p. 23). They additionally claim their tests show coaches are, "Highly success-driven men with an outstanding need to be on top" (1966, p. 22). What all this means in less academic terms is that coaches as a group are rather insensitive in their interpersonal relationships, and that, in an effort to produce winning teams, they will quite readily manipulate and exploit others. Furthermore, as Harry Edwards and the journalists I spoke of earlier have exposed, there is widespread racism in the coaching ranks. (Before I go on, I want to make myself very clear on one point. When I talk about racism among coaches, or Ogilvie and Tutko talk about authoritarianism among coaches, we are of course talking about coaches as a group. I fully recognize that there are many fine individuals in the coaching profession who do not conform to the group norm.)

Given what we know about coaches, I think we should be most careful who the coaches are with whom we choose to cooperate. It is inexcusable and socially irresponsible to put psychological information about athletes in the hands of the typical coach, for there is an excellent chance he will use this information, not to help athletes, but to further manipulate and exploit them. To provide a racist, authoritarian coach with psychological information about the athletes he is coaching can potentially have disastrous consequences for the athletes. There are hundreds of racist coaches throughout the country who would love to have "inside" psychological information about the black athletes they coach. Should we, as sport psychologists, provide them with this information? Quite obviously we should not, and those of you who have been doing this, especially if you plan to continue doing it, should realize that before too long the day will arrive when you will be held accountable for your actions.

I am not suggesting that sport psychologists should refuse to work with coaches who may be racist and/or authoritarian. Quite to the contrary, one of our prime concerns should be how we can best work with these kind of coaches to help them become more relaxed, sensitive human beings. However, we should not put psychological information about individual athletes in the hands of these men. We must establish priorities in our work, and when a coach behaves in a racist manner, our first priority should be to attenuate his racism, not to provide him with psychological information that will enable him to better manipulate and continue abusing black athletes.

The work of every social scientist has a value orientation, even though some individual social scientists may choose to ignore this reality. One cannot have a value neutral position. We are responsible for the social consequences of our work, and if we are going to provide coaches with psychological data that will facilitate their manipulating and handling of athletes, we must recognize the value orientation we are supporting.

Before getting into an analysis of *Problem Athletes and How to Handle Them,* I'm going to discuss briefly a matter that will have relevance to that analysis. What I want to talk about is the willingness, in fact many times the eagerness, of some social scientists to brand any individual that represents a threat to the status quo as a "problem." These social scientists feel that there must be something wrong with anyone who would have the audacity to challenge an authority figure. They are especially apt to feel this way if they happen to support and agree with the values of the authority figure who is being challenged. The most blatant use of this technique is in the Soviet Union where those individuals who represent a threat to the existing social order are declared mentally ill by the State's social scientists. After being declared mentally ill, they are then "hospitalized" for their own protection!

The value orientation of the Soviet psychologists and psychiatrists who perform this function is quite clear. They have made the assumption that conditions in contemporary Soviet society are such that any dissident individual who engages in protest activity must be mentally ill. We can readily recognize the value orientation of the Soviet social scientists, for many of us probably take just the opposite position, believing that any mentally healthy person should rebel against Soviet society because of what we would deem to be repressive social conditions.

Familiarity with the actions of Soviet social scientists should help to make us cognizant of the complexities involved in the placing of psychological or psychiatric labels on human beings. Hopefully, we, unlike the Soviet social scientists, will not diagnose someone as mentally ill, or even as a problem, simply because he represents a threat to the status quo or refuses to cooperate with certain authority figures. Before casting psychological labels on anyone, we must be familiar with the total social context in which he is operating. As Rollo May—a psychologist whose writings have had a significant impact on my own work—has pointed out, rebellious behavior under certain conditions "is not necessarily histrionic or evidence of a neurotic attitude. Indeed, there is reason for believing that it may represent the most mature form of distinctively human behavior" (*Man's Search for Himself,* 1967, p. 36).

It should be clear that only those psychologists whose value orientation is such that they are unequivocally committed to the perpetuation of the status quo will diagnose an individual as mentally ill or a problem simply because he poses a threat to the existing social order or challenges certain authority figures. An individual who is behaving in such a manner may very well have either minor or severe psychological problems, but rebellious behavior, in and of itself, is not sufficient cause for such a diagnosis.

Bringing this discussion back to the world of athletics, we should now recognize that though an athlete who refuses to submit to a coach certainly presents a problem for that coach, we must be very careful before we give "scientific" verification to the coach's labeling. The fact that a coach regards an athlete as a problem is not sufficient cause for a sport psychologist to label the athlete a problem unless, of course, the sport psychologist's value orientation is the same as that of the coach. A psychologist with a different value orientation might conclude that the coach is the problem, and the athlete's rebellious behavior is an intelligent, healthy response to the coach. For instance, racist coaches view proud black athletes who refuse to go docilely through their paces, jumping at the coaches' every command, as problems. My own value orientation is such that I would claim it is the racist coaches who are the problem and not rebellious black athletes. I would even go so far as to say that any committed, mentally healthy athlete, whether he be black, white, brown, or yellow, will resist manipulation by a racist coach.

In most cases, whether or not a sport psychologist will view an athlete as a problem is dependent on his value orientation. My fundamental criticism of Ogilvie and Tutko's work, especially as represented in *Problem Athletes and How to Handle Them,* is that they claim to be acting as value-free, objective social scientists, while in fact, they have totally adopted the value orientation of coaches as their own. Their working as the paid agents of coaches has apparently prevented them from seeing the coach-athlete relationship from any other perspective than that of the coach. Every one of the ten criteria that they list as a sign of an athlete resisting coaching and thus being susceptible to being labeled an "uncoachable" (1966, p. 33) is based on the assumption that any athlete who would not willingly cooperate with a coach is indeed a problem.

Nowhere in *Problem Athletes and How to Handle Them* do Ogilvie and Tutko adequately explain that there might be very rational reasons for athletes to rebel against certain coaches. In fact, given Ogilvie and Tutko's own description of what coaches as a group are like, it is not unreasonable to claim that the problem athletes are those who willingly submit themselves to authoritarian coaches, not those who are rebelling against these kind of coaches. If any group of athletes is a problem, it is those who are so authoritarian themselves that they can only respect and work with an authoritarian coach. I'm referring to those athletes who operate on such a low level of emotional and personal maturity that they feel it is necessary for their success as athletes to have a coach constantly forcing them to tow the line. These are the athletes who—as I pointed out earlier—will view openness or democratic behavior on the part of a coach as a sign of weakness.

Some of the criteria listed in *Problem Athletes and How to Handle Them* as a sign of athletes resisting coaching, especially when applied to high school and college athletes, demand schizophrenic-like behavior. According to Ogilvie and Tutko, athletes are resisting coaching and susceptible to being branded "uncoachable" when ". . . there is a tendency to be argumentative . . . ; the athlete will use other authorities in an attempt to refute the coach's arguments . . . ; they try to catch the coach making inconsistent statements and to find flaws in his arguments" (1966, p. 33). As I'm sure many of you recognize, these are some of the very qualities that most good teachers encourage in students. Yet high school and college athletes who behave in this manner with their coaches

—men who are supposed to be educators—often find themselves branded "uncoachables" or troublemakers by coaches who have read *Problem Athletes and How to Handle Them.*

Here's another criterion that Ogilvie and Tutko list in their book as a supposed indicator that an athlete is a potential "uncoachable": "These men tend to return to former coaches for support and instruction" (1966, p. 33). Now, if an athlete is willing to return to a former coach for help, this indicates that he at least does not have a phobic reaction toward coaches per se. He is simply discriminating against one particular coach with whom, for one reason or another, he is unable to get along. I personally know a number of track athletes who were fortunate enough to have very fine high school coaches. Less fortunately, the coaches at the colleges they chose to attend were extremely authoritarian. Not surprisingly, these athletes had a most difficult time getting along with their college coaches, and they frequently returned to their high school coaches for help and encouragement. To me, their behavior seemed most reasonable and rational, and indicated nothing about their coachability.

I fully recognize that there are some athletes whose psychological make-up prevents them from working with any coach. Those psychologists who label people might legitimately call this type of athlete an "uncoachable." But, once again, the very fact that an athlete is willing to return to a former coach for assistance indicates that he is not an "uncoachable," but simply finds one particular coach more to his liking than another.

Ogilvie and Tutko have developed one particular criterion of coachability that still amazes and amuses me whenever I think of it. I find it hard to take them seriously, but in a case study of an athlete they deemed to be "uncoachable," they actually say that one of the prime indicators of the athlete's uncoachability was his resistance and resentment toward taking their psychological battery of tests (1966, p. 36). They claim that ". . . outstanding athletes respond most favorably to the testing, once they have been informed that it is provided as a special service to be used only to enhance performance as an athlete" (1966, p. 36).

While resistance to taking Ogilvie and Tutko's tests is probably a sign of an athlete's intelligence and social awareness, it does not necessarily indicate anything about his coachability. To begin with, Ogilvie and Tutko cannot honestly assure athletes that coaches will use their data "only to enhance performance as an athlete," since they have no binding control over how coaches will use this data.

Let me describe a situation that frequently occurs on college track and field teams to illustrate my point. The team's top middle-distance runner has an excellent chance to win a national championship if he gauges his training so that he reaches his peak late in the season when the championship meets are held. Though the coach of course would like to see the athlete win a national championship, he is more concerned about having a successful dual meet season. Consequently, not only does he want the athlete to be in peak condition from early in the season, but he also expects him to compete in two and three events in each of the many dual meets on the team's schedule. From his experience the previous year, the athlete knows he will be exhausted by the time the championship meets come around if he accedes to the coach's demand.

Here is a clear conflict between an athlete's desire to fully develop his potential and a coach's desire to produce a winning team. In this situation, the typical coach will use any means at his disposal, including psychological data supplied to him by Ogilvie and Tutko, to manipulate and coerce the athlete into abandoning his own goal for the sake of the coach's desire to have a winning team. It would be a perfectly sane and intelligent response for our hypothetical runner to refuse to cooperate with Ogilvie and Tutko in this situation.

There are varied reasons why athletes might choose not to take psychological tests. Dave Meggyesy and Rick Sortun, two recently retired professional football players who played for the St. Louis Cardinals, refused to take the psychological battery of tests that were administered to the Cardinals during the 1969 season. Like Dr. Frank Ryan, the veteran NFL quarterback who recently refused to take these tests, they felt the tests were an invasion of privacy and were designed to give the team's owners and coaches information that might allow them to manipulate the players. Meggyesy and Sortun also refused to take the tests because they felt that if the owners were going to hire psychologists, it should have been to attenuate the racism on the team and not to manipulate the players. Professional football players are beginning to realize it is not in their best interests to cooperate with sport psychologists hired by the owners, and I predict that within a few years we'll see the Players Association take a stand against this practice.

Many athletes realize that Ogilvie and Tutko are working as the paid agent of coaches, even if they do not conceptualize it in those exact words. These athletes, quite correctly, see Ogilvie and Tutko as an extension of the coach. And if they are having problems with the coach, they are not likely to want to cooperate with agents of the coach, even though these agents claim to be value-free psychologists whose espoused aim is to help coaches and athletes. As long as Ogilvie and Tutko continue working as the agent of racist and/or authoritarian coaches, they can expect an ever increasing number of athletes to resist taking their battery of tests. When psychologists use psychology in the manner they have, all human beings, not only athletes, have good reason to resist and resent having to take psychological tests.

A frequent misuse of psychological testing is the resultant labeling of the individuals who took the tests. This practice often has unfortunate consequences. Among other things, labeling objectifies human beings and tends to prevent people from relating to the labeled individual as a "total person." The individual is reduced to a label and related to as say a paranoid rather than as a human being who has some problems. Despite the dehumanizing nature of this practice, some psychologists and psychiatrists are as quick as the mass media in their placing of labels on people.

Placing a negative psychological label on someone invariably assures that he will be denied certain opportunities. For example, in the American sports world, an athlete who is labeled an "uncoachable" is about as welcome as a person with V.D. at a Sexual Freedom League Party. But while there is good reason for preventing the person with V.D. from participating, there is no such reason for denying an "uncoachable" athlete the right to participate in sports. Still, this is what frequently happens, for as I mentioned earlier, having the "correct" attitude is often as important as athletic skill. Especially in team sports, coaches will usually quickly dismiss from the team any athlete who is deemed an "uncoachable." Once athletes acquire this label, coaches begin treating them as such, and consequently, as a result of coaches' hostile treatment, many of them eventually do become "uncoachable." Recognizing the possible consequences of our labeling an athlete an "uncoachable," I believe it is imperative that we re-evaluate the use of this and other similar labels.

As startling as it may seem to some of you, there are certain aspects of Ogilvie and Tutko's work that I believe many of us would do well to emulate. I especially admire them for their willingness to leave the security and serenity of the scientific laboratory and involve themselves in the "real world." While not denying the importance of laboratory work, I believe that more of us must be willing to involve ourselves in working with athletes, physical educators, and coaches. The significant problems facing the sports world will not be uncovered in scientific laboratories.

Although it probably seems that way to those of you who closely identify with coaches, I am not espousing a simple pro-athlete/anti-coach stance. I emphasize athletes' problems over those of coaches, not because athletes as a group are necessarily any more humane or just than coaches, but because they are the most powerless group in the social structure of organized athletics. They are the most powerless group, yet they are the individuals ostensibly for whose benefit we have athletics, at least in high school and college.

I believe there should be a democratic distribution of power in the sports world; one that would enable athletes to have a meaningful say in their sports participation. Most of my criticism of coaches stems from the fact that they, along with the administrators that support them, are totally resistant to giving up their totalitarian control over athletes. As I see it, my position, rather than being pro-athlete/anti-coach, is pro-democracy/anti-totalitarianism. Nearly all of our interscholastic and intercollegiate athletic programs are run in an authoritarian-totalitarian manner, and they cannot be expected to foster the development of democratic citizens. I am critical of anyone, whether he be an athlete, coach, or sports psychologist who supports and defends these programs.

In conclusion, let me remind you that science, both the social and physical sciences, can be used for man or against man—to manipulate and control man or to free him. We need only take a most cursory look at the world today for empirical evidence that science will not automatically work for man's benefit. Sport psychology is in its infancy, and it is still possible for us to have a significant influence on its growth. Like all other branches of the social sciences, sports psychology has the potential to develop into a tool of repression or a tool of liberation. The choice is up to you.

12
Drug Abuse and Athletics

One of the most critical issues the athletic world must face as we enter the 1970's is the problem of drug abuse. Athletes on the high school and college level as well as in the pros are being given steroids, amphetamines, painkillers, and most any other drug that seems to aid their performance with little or no concern being shown for the dangerous side-effects of these drugs. Bil Gilbert, in a three-part series for *Sports Illustrated,* exposed the rampant and widespread use of drugs in American athletics (June 23, 1969; June 30, 1969; July 7, 1969). In my opinion, Gilbert's series is one of the finest pieces of sports journalism ever written, and it is essential reading for anyone who hopes to understand the role sport plays in contemporary American society.

On October 20, 1970, a California State Legislative Sub-committee on Drug Abuse and Alcoholism held a hearing in Los Angeles, California, on drug abuse in athletics. This was the first official governmental inquiry into this problem in the history of American athletics. William Campbell, Chairman of the Sub-committee, issued the following statement:

Today the Assembly Health and Welfare Sub-committee on Drug Abuse and Alcoholism intends to explore the extent to which drugs play a part in athletic competition.

I'm sure those of you present today are aware of the publicity surrounding this issue. This publicity, if well founded, points to a potentially disasterous situation in athletics today, wherein the athlete—for real or imagined reasons—will feel the necessity to add drugs to his training regimen.

The fact that we are a drug-oriented society is a well established cliche: the fact that sports are now included within the context of a "turned on society" only confirms the extent to which chemicals are an inseparable aspect of American life.

Society's mass use of drugs in order to cope with the problems of living is serious indeed; the impact on athletics is even more alarming, for inappropriate drug use bears the seeds of destroying the notion of competition as we know it and as it has existed since the first Olympic Games.

There is no doubt that drugs have a definite role to play when required for the treatment of injury—and injury is an inevitable consequence of physical competition. When drugs assume a position of competitive importance beyond this role, however, the nature of competition and the role of sports in general becomes a perversion of its original purpose.

We have endeavored successfully to define distinctions regarding the use of drugs when horses compete against one another. I optimistically believe horse racing policies protect both the nature of competition and the health of the horse. I feel it is incumbent upon us, at this hearing today, to attempt to do no less for human competitors.

We at this hearing are sports fans, otherwise none of us probably would have expressed the obvious concern that is apparent by today's attendance. Working together with constructive suggestions we can prevent sports from becoming the testing battleground for chemical research. The medical laboratory, not the playing field, is the proper proving ground for testing drugs; and medical treatment of the ill, not the healthy athlete, is the proper role for the fruits of such research.

As Director of the Institute for the Study of Sport and Society, I was invited to testify at the hearing along with the following individuals: Dr. H. Kay Dooley, Athletic Consultant; Dr. Martin Blazina, U.C.L.A. Team Physician; Dr. Robert Kerlan, Los Angeles Lakers Team Physician; Dr. Eldor Siler, San Francisco Giants Team Physician; Dave Maggard, Track Coach at the University of California, Berkeley; Paul Lowe, a former All-pro football player; Robert Baxley, an attorney for professional athletes; and Dave Meggyesy, a former linebacker for the St. Louis Cardinals.

Not surprisingly, all those individuals who had a vested interest in the sports establishment testified that there was no real problem of drug abuse in athletics. Typical of this kind of testimony was that of Dave Maggard, head track coach at the University of California, Berkeley. Maggard told the legislators: "I don't feel that the problem as far as drug usage is as great a problem as some might suspect. . . . I don't think athletes, if they are involved with drug usage, are getting drugs from team physicians and trainers; this is something they are picking up someplace else. . . . I think that by and large the outstanding athletes in track and field are those who would not rely on this type of thing. . . . I think that the athlete who is looking for a crutch is the athlete who might be involved in this type of thing. I personally think that your real top notch—now I'm speaking here again about track and field—I don't think that the top notch athlete is involved in this to a great extent."[1]

The story the Los Angeles *Times* did on the hearing was typical of most press coverage. The *Times* story emphasized Maggard's testimony and that of the three or four other individuals who testified to the effect that there was no real problem of drug abuse in sport. Paul Lowe, Robert Baxley, Dave Meggyesy, and I testified that there is widespread drug abuse throughout almost all levels of athletic competition, yet there was not one mention of the nature of our testimony in the *Times* article. The following testimony of Paul Lowe is an example of what the *Times* piece ignored. In speaking about his years with the San Diego Chargers, Lowe said, "We had to take them [anabolic steroids] at lunch time. He [the trainer] would put them on a little saucer and prescribed for us to take them and if not he would suggest there might be a fine." Lowe, a former All-Pro running back, also mentioned he and most of his teammates regularly used amphetamines that were supplied by the Charger organization.

Other testimony ignored by the *Times* was that of Dave Meggyesy, a seven year veteran linebacker for the St. Louis Cardinals, and Robert Baxley, an attorney for professional football players. Baxley testified about the $1,250,000 suit he has filed against the San Diego Chargers on behalf of Houston Ridge, a former defen-

1. Dave Maggard's testimony and the testimony of others quoted in the text was taken from the official transcript of the proceedings released by the Sub-committee shortly after the Los Angeles hearing.

sive tackle for the Chargers. He described the Ridge suit to the legislators: "The complaint is essentially for malpractice. One aspect of the complaint is for battery, for the administration of what are termed 'dangerous drugs' under the Business and Professions Code, and the third cause of action is for conspiracy involving the American Football League and the National Football League for their participation in the use of the drug."

Dave Meggyesy spoke of the widespread use of drugs in professional football in general and on his former team in particular: "The trainer of the Cardinals had what amounted to a drugstore down in his training room. The drug cabinets were open and could be used by any of the players. . . . They extensively used cortisone, xylocain, and novacain to shoot injured ballplayers up before the game."

The remainder of this chapter is an edited version of my testimony before the Sub-committee. I have based the text on the official transcript of the proceedings.

MR. SCOTT: One of the top priorities of the Institute for the Study of Sport and Society since the Institute was founded last spring has been what we feel is the crisis in drug usage in sport. I think that by now both popular journalism as well as scholarly research have shown that there is a very real and urgent problem in this area. I think that most of us here who do not have a vested interest in the sports industry will accept that the problem exists.

ASSEMBLYMAN TOWNSEND: I'm sorry, Mr. Scott—excuse me, Mr. Chairman—did you say this is a top priority item with the Institute?

MR. SCOTT: That's correct. As soon as the funds are available, one of the first research projects the Institute will conduct will be an inquiry into the use of drugs in sports.

ASSEMBLYMAN TOWNSEND: So that in your opinion it's pretty prevalent?

MR. SCOTT: That's correct.

ASSEMBLYMAN TOWNSEND: Thank you.

MR. SCOTT: The first question we all have to deal with is the reliability of data in the area of drug usage in sport. I'd like to mention briefly two incidents that illustrate why it is so difficult to get reliable information on this problem. Last year, the University of California team physician, speaking at a medical conference in San Francisco, mentioned that if any members of the Cal football team were involved in the use of amphetamines that at most it was only a few players. He emphasized that any usage was very isolated, that it was not at all widespread. The team physician voiced the attitude of the Cal athletic establishment.

On the other hand, a student who was a football player at Cal, a young man named Mike Mohler, did a research paper for a course I was teaching at the University of California at Berkeley last year. Mr. Mohler interviewed practically every varsity football player on the Cal team. The results of Mohler's study were eventually published in the San Francisco *Examiner*. Among other things, Mohler found that approximately half of the Cal players had used or were using amphetamines while playing football. His study also showed that 28% of the players had used anabolic steroids. Shortly after the results of Mohler's study were published, an attempt was made by officials of the Cal athletic department to discredit it—an earlier attempt had been made by these same individuals to get Mohler to not allow his study to be released publicly. The Bay Area press talked to numerous Cal athletes about Mohler's study, and almost all of the athletes agreed with his findings. From their perspective as participants, the athletes seemed to feel that Mohler's data were reliable. In fact, I personally saw many Cal athletes thank Mohler for having the courage to resist the pressure the athletic department had put on him not to publicly release his findings. The athletes were grateful to Mohler because they thought the matter was something that should be brought before the public.

The other incident I'd like to relate to you involves the use of steroids at the University of California. The head football coach, Ray Willsey, claims that neither he nor his staff have been involved in getting athletes to use anabolic steroids. "The only items supplied to the athletes," according to Willsey, "are food supplements to aid body building and sleeping pills the night before a game if an athlete has trouble getting to sleep" (Berkeley *Gazette,* May 12, 1970, p. 9).

Jim Calkins, the co-captain of Willsey's 1969 Cal football

team, disagrees with his former coach. According to Calkins, "A coach recommended to me to take gianabol—an anabolic steroid —to increase my weight" (Berkeley *Gazette,* May 12, 1970, p. 10). On the coach's suggestion, Calkins went to the team physician who put him on steroids. Calkins gained weight and got stronger as the coach had told him he would, but he also began to experience some bad side-effects after using the drug for about twenty-five days. He went back to see the team physician who admitted that these kind of side-effects sometimes do occur and took him off the drug. Calkins has since acknowledged on a number of occasions that this incident was the beginning of his disillusionment with coaches and big-time college athletics. I might add that I have also talked with numerous other Cal football players besides Calkins who claim the football coaches sent them to the team physician for the express purpose of getting a prescription for steroids.

CHAIRMAN CAMPBELL: Mr. Duffy has a question.

ASSEMBLYMAN DUFFY: Are team physicians the same for football as for track?

MR. SCOTT: Yes. They have one team physician.

ASSEMBLYMAN DUFFY: Thank you.

MR. SCOTT: My personal observation is that there is a tremendous amount of hypocrisy in this area. If coaches and athletic administrators were as concerned about steroid and amphetamine use as they are about athletes drinking beer or smoking marijuana, the problem could be eliminated almost overnight. Unfortunately, most coaches show little or no real concern about the use of amphetamines and steroids as long as these drugs seem to be helping them to produce winning teams.

I covered the Mexico City Olympic Games as a journalist, and in talking with athletes from all over the world, and particularly top American track and field stars, the discussions on drug use did not involve whether or not athletes were taking drugs, but what kind of drugs they were taking. Athletes debated which type of anabolic steroid was best and what kind of amphetamine could go undetected in the drug tests being administered by Olympic officials. It was not a question of whether or not they were taking drugs, but of which drugs were best to take. It is widely recognized

JIM CALKINS, co-captain of the 1969 University of California football team and recipient of an NCAA postgraduate fellowship: "You see many black athletes speaking out about the injustices, but the white players are gutless. They don't want to take a stand. They are so entrenched in the system and so full of all this superpatriotic stuff" (*Courtesy of the University of California Athletic Department*).

in track and field circles that it is next to impossible to get to the top in most weight events and the decathlon without the use of these drugs since most of the top athletes are using them.

The widespread use of drugs by Olympic athletes and professional athletes is well known to high school and college athletes and their coaches. And since high school and college coaches and athletes use the more accomplished Olympic stars and professional athletes as models, it is not unreasonable to assume that before long the problem of drug usage will be as critical in our high schools and colleges as it now is on the Olympic and professional levels. For instance, the typical college football coach does not perceive of himself as an educator—at least not in the sense that a college professor might. In other words, the model that he uses for his behavior is not that of an educator, but that of a professional football coach.

ASSEMBLYMAN CAMPBELL: Let me interject here. You're suggesting, then, that what occurred at the Olympics was the fact that people were by-and-large using drugs and the discussions down there were not the fact that they were using drugs, but what kind of drugs to use, what would be the best, and what would escape detection. Is that correct?

MR. SCOTT: That's correct.

ASSEMBLYMAN CAMPBELL: And you're suggesting that because the high school player tends to look up to the Olympic athlete or professional athlete where drug abuse is very common, that he tends to mimic these kinds of activities—using amphetamines, steroids, etc.

MR. SCOTT: Yes, that's exactly what I'm suggesting.

Let me make it clear, however, that I am not espousing a simple anti-drug stand. The issue of drug usage by athletes is much too complicated, in my opinion, to take a blind stand either for or against drugs. The intelligent, responsible use of drugs can be a legitimate part of sports medicine just as the use of antibiotics is a legitimate part of general medical practice. The main problem with drug usage in athletics today is that athletes are using drugs that are known to have dangerous side-effects and other drugs of which there is little or no knowledge about what their long range effects may be. This kind of drug abuse has no place in sport.

However, if sports medicine can come up with some drugs that facilitate the healing process, for instance, while having no dangerous side effects, then I personally would have no objection to the use of these drugs. For example, if a track athlete who had trained for years and finally made it to the Olympic Games received an injury shortly before Olympic competition, I see nothing wrong with him being allowed to use a drug that could facilitate the healing of his injury as long as studies had shown this drug had no dangerous side-effects.

You have asked individuals testifying at this hearing to offer suggestions for what can be done to prevent drug abuse in sport, and I'd like to address this question before concluding my testimony. I think it would be a mistake for you to take a purely legalistic approach to the problem. Drug abuse is only a symptom of the dehumanizing conditions that exist in American athletics. Something that the Institute for the Study of Sport and Society is doing, and perhaps your committee can also do, is to look into the philosophy that dominates American athletics—the philosophy that has fostered the conditions that exist today with regard to drug usage and the many other problems plaguing sport. You might want to, as the Institute is also doing, look into who the organizations and men are who control athletics in America. I suggest you do this, for as I'm sure you know—whether it be drug abuse in sport or in other areas of society—a purely legalistic approach is not enough. It simply cannot control the situation. Drug abuse is only one of the many symptoms that show that something is terribly wrong with the role sport is playing in society today, and if you are serious about doing something to correct this problem, you will have to look at the root causes and not focus just on this one symptom.

PART III

SPORT, EDUCATION, AND SOCIETY

The competitions and contests, the delight in bodily activity, the loyalties, and the honor that form a part of that vast organism called college athletics are the reflections in our college life of characteristics that are common to the youth of the world. In the pages that follow, these and other less pleasing phenomena of college athletics will be examined in the hope that those aspects which are good may in course of time achieve an unassailable predominance over those which are less worthy to survive. There can be no question of abolishing college athletics, nor should there be. What can be looked for is a gradual establishment through concrete action of a few general principles, to which all men would agree in the abstract. But even this slow change will be impossible without the sanction of an enlightened college and public opinion.

CARNEGIE FOUNDATION REPORT ON
ATHLETICS AND HIGHER EDUCATION (1929)

13

A Look at the Past

In attempting to understand the role athletics play in contemporary American education, it is helpful to take a historical look at the role that physical education and athletics have played in formal education in Western culture. Most contemporary social ills have their origins in the past, and the malaise that affects physical education and athletic activities within our schools today is no exception. The brief historical sketch set forth here will not do justice to the complexities involved in the role athletics played in each period examined—an entire book would be needed for that —but it should facilitate an understanding of the problems facing us today.

Prior to the sixth century B.C., there were two main athletic traditions in Greece; the Spartan tradition which emphasized the militaristic value of sport and the Athenian tradition which emphasized the artistic nature of athletics. Sparta was an aggressive city-state and used sport primarily as a training ground for its warriors. Athletes from both Sparta and Athens performed most credibly in the ancient Olympic Games, thus documenting the fact that both a militaristic approach emphasizing authoritarian discipline and a more artistic approach emphasizing self-discipline could produce highly skilled athletes.

The Athenian tradition finally prevailed, and at no time during the history of Western civilization have physical education and athletics been a more integral part of formal education than they were in Greece from approximately the sixth century to the fourth century B.C. Whether it was because of noble esthetic and philosophical considerations or simply because their very survival often depended on physical fitness, athletics and physical education were inextricably involved in Greek education during this period. The Greeks were concerned with developing the whole man, both mind and body, and any form of one-sided development was anathema. It was not at all unusual for the same person to be involved in the teaching of both an academic subject and physical education. Plato was perhaps the most well known teacher who was also a fine athlete; he often spent much of his time instructing students in the art of wrestling. In a statement which reveals the educational ethos of this period, Plato observed, "The mere athlete becomes too much of a savage, and the mere musician is melted and softened beyond what is good for him—the two should therefore be blended in right proportions" (quoted in Moore, 1966, p. 6).

The Greeks believed there was nothing shameful about the human body, and nudity within the schools was common. A handsomely developed physique was as valued as a cultivated mind, but the ideal was the harmonious development of mind and body. Even the performers in the ancient Greek Olympic Games often were required to write poetry or exhibit other artistic talent along with their athletic feats. Throughout this period, physical education and athletics were primarily for the enjoyment and self-development of the individuals involved in these activities, and except for the Olympic Games, spectator interest was very minimal.[1]

The emphasis on athletics for athletes began to decline during the Hellenistic period, and with the rise of Rome, the era of mass-spectator sports blossomed. Lucrative prizes became common, and sport took on a spectator rather than participant orientation. Professionalization became rampant—many individuals concentrated solely on physical development—and the ideal of developing the whole man was forgotten. Sport, instead of being an integral part

---

1. It is important to note that the education of the whole man, both mind and body, was an education that was not extended to the masses—most of whom were slaves.

of education for all healthy young people, became the privilege of those relatively few individuals who possessed sufficient athletic talent to perform as professional athletes. While this period commercialized sport and ushered in the rise of professionalism, no real antipathy developed between those involved in scholarly pursuits and those involved in athletic ones. Although little thought was given to developing the whole man, athletics and scholarship had not yet become mutually exclusive activities. This development—the consequences of which are still much in evidence today—did not occur until the Middle Ages and the rise of the Christian Church.

Education was administered and governed by the Church throughout the Middle Ages, and as the noted British classics scholar H. A. Harris points out, "The education given by the priests and monks was exclusively literary" (1964, p. 193). Concern for the physical was at first considered sinful, but even after the Manichaean heresy with its contempt for the human body was rejected by the Church, physicalness and athletics were still frowned upon. Life was to be endured rather than enjoyed, and most of man's efforts were directed to securing passage to heaven. The body was nothing more than the temporal carrier of the soul, and efforts to develop it were at best viewed as frivolous. The development of the mind and body were considered to be inimical pursuits.

But the Church needed soldiers to protect its prerogatives, and although physical education was not a part of formal education, it did play an important role in the training of warriors. Scholars, who were carrying on God's work through literary pursuits and the exclusive cultivation of the mind, looked with great disdain at the warriors, who were enraptured with the cult of physicalness. And the warriors, many of whom probably felt it was their services that allowed God's work to be carried on, privately, and sometimes publicly, talked about the emaciated scholars with great contempt.

The Renaissance began to loosen the monolithic control of the Church, and a number of Renaissance educators tried to revive the long dormant ideal of developing the whole man, both mind and body. But although school children indulged themselves in playing games, physical education and athletics did not become an integral part of formal education during this period.

Jean Jacques Rousseau tackled the problem of the dichotomy between physical and mental development in *Emile,* his famous treatise on education. Rousseau's insightfulness was such that much of his work is still relevant today—at least in spirit if not in specifics—and his observations on physical education are no exception. Rousseau wrote the following while discussing what role "the training of the body" should play in the education of his imaginary pupil, Emile: ". . . it is a shocking blunder to imagine that physical exercise is injurious to the operation of the mind; as if the two kinds of activity did not proceed together, with the mind always directing the body. . . . The more his body is exercised the better his mind becomes. Strength and reason develop together and help each other" (Boyd, 1965, p. 53). And across the Atlantic in the fledgling United States, Thomas Jefferson, writing some twenty years after *Emile* was first published in 1762, also addressed the same problem. "Knowledge indeed is desirable, a lovely possession, but I do not scruple to say that health is more so. It is of little consequence to store the mind with science if the body be permitted to become debilitated. If the body be feeble, the mind will not be strong" (Lee, 1961, p. 143).

Despite the efforts of Rousseau, Jefferson, and other Enlightenment writers during the eighteenth century, it was not until the middle of the nineteenth century that physical education once again became a part of formal education as it was in the days of ancient Greece. This development occurred in the exclusive public schools and universities of England—Eton, Westminster, Rugby, Shrewsbury, Harrow, Charterhouse, Winchester, Oxford, and Cambridge. The English were captivated primarily by what they believed to be the character building value of athletics. It was the publication of *Tom Brown's Schooldays* in 1857, a book written by Thomas Hughes, which did the most to popularize the notion that athletics could play an important role in the moral development of young people. Two well known Englishmen, Philip Goodhart, M.P., and Christopher Chataway, discuss the influence of Hughes' work in their own book, *War Without Weapons:* ". . . the notion popularised by *Tom Brown's Schooldays* that sport nourished virtue now embellished games playing with a new respectability, and the advent of respectability meant that the enormous organising ability of the solid Victorian middle class could now be applied to sport" (1968, p. 28).

The "enormous organising ability of the solid Victorian middle class" was applied to sport, and so was its puritanical, bourgeois approach to life. Unlike the ancient Greeks, the English did not view the athlete as a legitimate artist who expressed himself through his sports performance; they definitely were not interested in the athlete experiencing joy from the coordinated and often rhythmic movement of his body, and neither did they want him to take pride in a handsomely developed physique. Sports taught the middle- and upper-class youths attending the public schools how to stoically endure pain, how to persevere through the most extreme adversity, how to keep physically fit, and how to gain more "worthwhile" rewards by learning to delay immediate gratification. Simply put, it was believed that athletics taught stern-faced British youths discipline and helped to develop leadership ability. Britannia ruled not only the waves but much of the world during the nineteenth century, and the many officers needed for her ubiquitous military forces received their early training on the playing fields of Oxford, Cambridge, and the various preparatory schools.

As you will discover in the following chapters, all of these various traditions have, in one way or another, had an influence on the growth and development of athletics within our schools and colleges.

14

The Growth and
Development of
Intercollegiate Athletics

The Greek (Athenian) tradition of athletics for athletes has had no significant impact on the growth of physical education and athletics in American education. To be sure, some conscientious physical educators during the eighteenth century struggled most admirably to revive this tradition and make it an integral part of education in the United States, but their pleas were met with either indifference or contempt from those who controlled the schools and colleges of colonial America. Almost all educational institutions of this period were controlled or dominated by the clergy, and these men still labored under the medieval belief about the frivolity of physical pursuits. In 1787 the faculty at Princeton even went so far as to prohibit students from playing shinty, a game similar to modern baseball (Savage, 1929, pp. 14–15). A few humanistic physical educators are still espousing the Greek ideal today, but so far their efforts have usually been to no avail, and there is little indication that their ideas will be given serious consideration in the foreseeable future.

By the early nineteenth century, increasing numbers of young people began attending schools and colleges; and as usually happens despite the protestations of adults when youth gather in large numbers, they played and enjoyed themselves. This games-playing eventually developed into rather loosely organized but intensely competitive athletic contests between the various classes within the schools and colleges. Faculties, when not prohibiting physical activities, ignored them, and almost all athletic contests of this period were organized by students for their own enjoyment.

Along with concomitant educational changes, the industrialization and urbanization of the United States in the latter half of the nineteenth century helped to create a social climate which fostered the growth of organized sport, and the first formal interscholastic and intercollegiate athletic contests took place in the 1860's (Savage, 1929, p. 17). High school football matches began in the public and private schools of Boston during this period, and in 1869 college football began with the inaugural game between Princeton and Rutgers. American schools and colleges followed the pattern of Oxford and Cambridge during the beginning years of interscholastic and intercollegiate competition, and the responsibility for organizing athletic programs remained in the hands of undergraduates.

Howard Savage, in his comprehensive history of college athletics written in 1929 for the Carnegie Foundation For the Advancement of Teaching, sets 1880 as the date when the professionalization of American intercollegiate athletics commenced (p. 21). *But long before then the door was left open for commercialization when colonial educators had refused to make physical education and athletics an integral part of education.* Savage chose 1880 because sports pages began to appear in the daily newspapers then, and college administrators and boards of trustees immediately recognized the favorable publicity their colleges could receive from newspaper stories chronicling the exploits of successful athletic teams. Almost overnight college sports became a serious business, and their management could no longer remain in the hands of irresponsible undergraduates; at least that is the way those administrators who refused to give physical education a meaningful role in their schools' curriculum but welcomed the professional coach saw the matter.

Church-controlled colleges which had up to this time condemned physical activity as frivolous did an about-face, and "Intercollegiate athletics at Notre Dame were consciously developed in
the 1890s as an agency of student recruitment" (Rudolph, 1962,
p. 385). A few colleges resisted the advance of professionalization
by de-emphasizing sports or withdrawing from intercollegiate athletic competition altogether. But this type of principled behavior
was foreign to most college administrators back then just as it
would be today, and they did not persist in it for long. "By 1900
the relationship between football and public relations had been
firmly established and almost everywhere acknowledged as one of
the sport's major justifications" (Rudolph, 1962, p. 385). To this
day, athletics is the only university-sponsored activity that is recorded almost daily in American newspapers as well as on radio
and television.

James Reston, though showing little concern for the effects
professionalized college athletics may have on the participants, succinctly summarizes most of the financial benefits to be gained from
the publicity resulting from a "successful" athletic program (quoted
in Goodhart and Chataway, 1968, p. 86):

No doubt state university sport has been professionalised and
corrupted, but it has done something else. It has produced football
teams which have become symbols of state pride. It has kept alumni
in touch with the university. More important, it has held the interest
and the allegiance of legislators in the state capitols and has in the
process helped produce educational appropriations for all these land
grant institutions on a scale that would never have been possible
without the attraction and the pride engendered by these sporting
events at the universities on autumn Saturday afternoons.

But as Myles Jackson points out in an article in *Fortune*
magazine (December, 1962), these benefits do not come cheaply.
After examining big-time college football in the early 1960's, *Fortune* estimated that $400,000 is a minimum yearly outlay needed
to field a big-time college football team. The financial risks involved in this operation have become so enormous that college

football programs are now run like industrial corporations, and as David Riesman and Reuel Denny make clear in their article "Football in America: A study in Cultural Diffusion," ". . . the game is now a cooperative enterprise in which mistakes are too costly —to the head coach, the budget, even the college itself—to be left to individual initiative" (1951, p. 318). These financial pressures have resulted in the game being taken away from the players to such an extent that John Reaves, the University of Florida quarterback and the nation's number one passer during the 1969 season, began protesting during the fall of 1970 that he felt "like a robot" since the Florida coach, Doug Dickey, was calling all the plays (St. Petersburg *Times,* September 19, 1970, p. 1C). The pressures Riesman and Denny mention are operating even in the Ivy League. Harvard lost its star quarterback, Frank Champi, after the second game of the 1969 season when he suddenly quit because football was ". . . too mechanized. It doesn't allow for the human being. . . . We're like pieces of machinery. . . . The whole concept of machine sports was just stopping me (*Sport,* December, 1969, p. 4). And football coaches all over the country— both in the pros as well as college—are beginning to discover that Steve Champi and John Reaves are not rarities. Three top professional players, Dave Meggyesy, Rick Sortun, and Chip Oliver, recently retired at the height of their careers, and the University of Pennsylvania lost its leading ground-gainer and three other top players halfway through the 1970 season when they suddenly quit. One of them accused the Penn coach of "taking all the fun out of football" (New York *Times,* Oct. 10, 1970, p. 30). And press reports throughout the fall of 1970 showed that scores of other college football players were refusing to play football for similar reasons.

Even the very finest college football players are beginning to question the relevance of big-time college football. Steve Owens, the 1969 Heisman Trophy winner, talked about the pressures of major college football shortly before the end of his last season at Oklahoma. "In high school the game was almost entirely fun," he told a reporter from *Sport* magazine. "Here it's a business. We're suppose to fill that stadium with 60,000 fans and win. . . . I still

STEVE OWENS, 1969 Heisman Trophy winner and now a professional football star for the Detroit Lions: "In high school the game was almost entirely fun. Here [at Oklahoma] it's a business. We're supposed to fill that stadium with 60,000 fans and win. . . . I still love the game, but there's so much pressure, sometimes it makes me wonder." (*Photo courtesy University of Oklahoma Athletic Department*).

love the game, but there's so much pressure, sometimes it makes me wonder (*Sport,* November, 1969, p. 94).[1]

The financial pressures of big-time college athletics exert themselves in myriad ways, not the least of which is the annual recruiting extravaganza that sends college coaches scurrying all over the country taking high school athletic stars out for steak dinners (see Randy Smyth's excellent article on recruiting in Chapter 6). The typical assistant football or basketball coach spends well over 50% of his working hours on recruiting—an activity that has no reasonable educational justification. Recruiting does, however, have a financial justification, for as most any coach will tell you, "If you don't get the studs to begin with, no amount of coaching will get you a winner." Almost needless to say, it's winning teams that make money for athletic departments.

An entire book could be written chronicling the deals that have been made by coaches in an effort to recruit outstanding high school athletes, but one of the most brazen and flagrantly commercial incidents occurred during the winter of 1969 when the University of Maryland athletic department began placing ads in the Washington *Post* exhorting four Washington, D.C. area high school basketball stars to enroll at Maryland (San Francisco *Chronicle,* April 2, 1969, p. 50). At Ohio State, the coaches spend

1. Jim Calkins, the captain of the 1969 University of California football team, goes well beyond Owens in his questioning of the values of college football (Padwe, 1970, p. 67):
When I first came to California, I'd do anything for the coach. I'd take what he said as the word, without question. Now, I've come to the conclusion that I better start saying something. That's been part of the problem. You see so many black athletes speaking out now. But the white players are gutless. They don't want to take a stand. They are so entrenched in the system and so full of all this super-patriotic stuff. So the coach is all-dominant, all-powerful. I've never seen one player call a coach a bleephead like they call us all the time. And nobody ever questions their training methods, the way they run us into the ground, the drugs they give us.
Sometimes I look inside myself and think I won't be leaving with my dignity because of what I had to go through. The most degrading thing is being treated like a child. I was programmed to act and function in a certain way. And they talk about learning things from football. I don't think I learned a thing. The attitude is that you're getting paid to play football so you can't gripe. If that's the way they want it, fine. BUT I SAY TO THEM, YOU DON'T PAY ENOUGH.

so much time talking to high school recruits on the phone that the athletic department has a yearly phone bill of $27,000. And the University of Texas spends over $50,000 a year just to finance the recruiting efforts of their coaching staff (Wolfe, June, 1970, p. 68).

The absence of any meaningful role for women in intercollegiate athletics is another indication of the overriding influence finances have on the operation of college athletic programs. Women's sports have little spectator appeal for the American public, and thus would not generate any significant revenue for athletic departments. When American women can dominate the Olympic Games in sports such as swimming and to a lesser extent in track and field, it is both dishonest and irresponsible to say—as most male athletic directors do—that it is because of a lack of ability and interest among women that they are not given a significant role in intercollegiate athletics.

The distinction that is made between major and minor sports in nearly all intercollegiate athletic programs is yet another indication that financial considerations override educational concerns in the operation of these programs. In reality, major sports turn out to be those activities that are profit-making, i.e., football and basketball, while minor sports are usually non-profit making activities, i.e., swimming, tennis, gymnastics. Football and basketball have a role to play in any intercollegiate athletic program, but there is no educational justification for these two activities to consume well over 50% of the total athletic budget, as they do at nearly all major colleges and universities today.

An incident that occurred a few years ago at the University of California at Berkeley further illustrates the emphasis placed on major versus minor sports. Involved in the incident were Dan Milman, a member of the Cal gymnastics team, and Ray Willsey, Cal's head football coach and assistant athletic director. During his four years at Cal, Milman had won a world championship in trampoline competition, All-American honors for three years, an NCAA championship, and was captain of the Cal team that won the NCAA championship his senior year. Quite understandably, Milman was well known on the Berkeley campus, for he had received a tremendous amount of publicity on the sports pages of

DEBBIE MEYER, World Record holder and Olympic champion swimming star (*Wide World Photos*).

WYOMIA TYUS, winning 100 meter dash at the Tokyo Olympics. Wyomia's teammate, Edith McGuire, (second from left), was second. (*Wide World Photos*).

the school newspaper as well as other San Francisco Bay Area newspapers. Less than a month after he had graduated from Cal, Milman visited the athletic director's office in an effort to pick up his senior letterman award. The athletic director was not in, so he was sent to see Ray Willsey, the assistant athletic director. Willsey told Milman that he did not know who he was—he could be someone who had just walked in off the street—and that he could not give him his award without a signed note from the gymnastics coach.

Those relatively few colleges that still manage to reap a financial profit from football and basketball often use these profits to finance non-paying intercollegiate athletic activities, the so-called minor sports. In a classical *non sequitur,* athletic directors use this example of benevolence as a rationale for justifying their professionalized football and basketball programs. Although the athletic director's reasoning may make no sense to logicians, acamedicians, or critics of professionalized intercollegiate athletics, it makes a great deal of sense to administrators, trustees, and state legislators —men who are usually more concerned with finances than with education. As long as college athletics can be a self-supporting activity, most administrators, and nearly all legislators, are not going to advocate financing athletics on the same basis as a regular academic activity, *regardless of what the educational consequences of a professionalized athletic program may be.*

Most colleges today—including those with professionalized athletic programs—do not have totally self-supporting athletic departments. It is not unusual for athletic departments to receive a large subsidy taken from student fees. For example, at the University of California at Berkeley the athletic department each year receives approximately $309,000 appropriated from student registration fees. In addition, Berkeley students still must pay for a student activity card if they want to attend Cal athletic contests.

Despite the fact that many athletic departments receive this type of subsidy, according to Jackson's *Fortune* article mentioned earlier, Cornell, which had an athletic department deficit of $313,-000 in 1961, is typical of a college with a major athletic program. This is quite a contrast to the past; for example, in 1928 Yale's athletic program grossed $1,119,000 and netted over $348,500

(Savage, 1929, p. 87). Thus, it is obvious that financial profit is no longer the sole justification for professionalized college athletics. Excluding the already discussed benefits derived from the publicity resulting from a successful athletic team, there are numerous other non-pecuniary benefits.

Athletics, ever since 1900, have been the one activity that has been able to serve as a basis for campus unity. Community at colonial colleges was based on a common religious belief, and later it stemmed from a search for "truth" and knowledge under the guise of a liberal arts curriculum. But all this ended by 1910 with the decline of religious emphasis and the break-up of the university into academic departments and the concomitant rise of the elective curriculum. Today scholarly pursuits may serve as a basis for community at Reed or St. Johns (Md.), but at most American colleges from Yale and Harvard to Southern California and Alabama, intercollegiate athletics is the only activity that can unite on a regular basis a broad cross-section of the entire academic community: professors, students, college employees, and alumni. An example of this is Notre Dame where community is built around the fighting Irish football team, not St. Augustine's "City of God" or some other metaphysical concept.

All social units, from families to nations, need unity to survive, and it is only natural that society will appropriately reward those individuals who create and maintain social unity. Thus, it should come as no surprise to learn that at many American colleges the football coach is paid more than any regular academic professor. Paul "Bear" Bryant, the legendary football coach was told he he could name his own salary when Alabama offered him the head football coaching position a number of years ago. Bryant first inquired as to what salary Alabama's president was paid. He then humbly requested one slightly less, for he did not believe it was proper for the football coach to be paid more than the president. In reality, however, Bryant's income including fringe benefits far exceeds the president's. Though their rationale differs, contemporary radicals of both the left and the right are correct when they speak of the failure of our colleges and universities. This failure is only dramatized by the fact that professionalized college athletics, and all its concomitant values, is the only activity serving as a basis

for community on the campuses of our institutions of higher learning.

Athletic departments, perhaps feeling a little self-conscious
about their prominent role in university communities, eventually
began to look around for other justifications for their enterprise.
They quickly hit upon the British tradition popularized by *Tom
Brown's Schooldays.* Coaches were not only filling the coffers and
gaining favorable publicity by turning out winning teams; they were
also building character and preserving the moral fiber of the country on which our very survival as a nation depended! Under the
firm hand and watchful eye of The Coach, young boys were being
molded into men. Students who resisted being molded were, and
still are today, labelled "troublemakers" and quickly filtered out of
interscholastic and intercollegiate athletic programs. As I will discuss more fully in Chapter 16, the morality coaches teach is one
that emphasizes tradition, authoritarian discipline, automatic respect for authority, and other conservative values that meet with
the approval of the alumni—the controlling force behind most
major athletic programs.

Besides being a training ground for molding young boys into
citizens who will be rubber stamps for the on-going social fiction
and being a means for gaining a college favorable publicity, sports
also perform another possibly even more reactionary service. Athletic contests—from Little League baseball to professional football
—bring some temporary excitement and meaning into the often
meaningless, lonely lives of all too many middle-aged American
males. A dull, insignificant job can be more easily endured if one is
able to spend evenings and weekends watching exciting sports
events. As Professor Harry Edwards says, "If there is a religion in
this country today, it is sports." Two conservative Englishmen,
Philip Goodhart and Christopher Chataway, recognize the role
sport plays in modern society (1968, p. 156):

The growing passion for sport may be seen as a sad commentary
on the inadequacy of the societies we have created. It is only
because millions of people are not effectively involved in the societies
in which they live and work that they identify themselves so pas-
sionately with the participants in some sporting ritual. As work

HARRY EDWARDS, assistant professor in the department of sociology at the University of California, Berkeley. Edwards was a standout basketball and track and field athlete at San Jose State College. After receiving his A.B. degree, Edwards was awarded a Woodrow Wilson Fellowship to Cornell University where he earned his Ph.D. In the author's opinion, Edwards' brilliant and committed leadership of the black athlete revolt was the most significant event in the American **athletic world during the 1960's** (*Photo courtesy Micki Scott*).

becomes even less satisfying, and as the feeling of being a cog in an impersonal machine spreads farther, the ranks of the eager spectators are sure to swell.

But Goodhart and Chataway also recognize that if the ranks of spectators do not swell, the ranks of those pleading for social justice and a meaningful life might; thus, they are not really upset over the rise of mass spectator sports.

Today, with a nation's vitality often measured by the accomplishments of its youths in the international athletic arena, college athletic programs are being used as training grounds for the development of what could be called athletic gladiators. When famous college athletes such as Jim Ryun and Lew Alcindor decided not to participate in certain international sporting events, the American press almost unanimously denounced them as ingrates and traitors. Since they were given athletic scholarships and had been able to train using the world's best athletic facilities, the press felt they had a responsibility to represent the United States.

Most international sports competition involves only amateur athletes, and since almost all major athletic activities outside of our schools and colleges are professional, interscholastic and intercollegiate athletic programs are the only real training grounds we have for preparing our athletic warriors. Nearly every United States athlete on our Olympic track and field, basketball, swimming, and gymnastic teams in Mexico City was attending, or had attended, college on an athletic scholarship. One may justifiably question, however, why our colleges are concerned with preparing international sports competitors, especially when this preparation usually conflicts with espoused educational goals.

Physical fitness benefits are a frequent claim made on behalf of college athletics. While this argument is not without some merit, it is quickly becoming suspect as the number of serious injuries among athletes continues to increase at an epidemic rate. There are few individuals who have seriously participated in college athletics who do not have permanent injuries as a result of their sports participation. Furthermore, there is no indication that college athletes are more likely than non-athletes to maintain a reasonable level of physical fitness after their competitive athletic careers are finished. This should not come as any surprise since the major intercollegiate sports are not activities one is likely to be able to continue participating in after college graduation. Additionally, the widespread use of steroids, amphetamines, and other dangerous drugs by athletes is certainly not a positive contribution to physical fitness (see Chapter 12).

Psychoanalyst Robert Moore, in his book, *Sports and Mental Health,* mentions what he and others who view man as an innately aggressive animal believe to be an invaluable function of sport. "Sports and recreation," according to Dr. Moore, "are particularly valuable as a means of partial outlet of aggressive and sexual impulses whether we are participant or observer" (1966, p. 74). And Konrad Lorenz, though his view of sport is not as simplistic as Moore's, still believes, ". . . the main function of sport today lies in the cathartic discharge of aggressive urge . . ." (1966, p. 271).

There can be little argument that strenuous physical exercise, especially body-contact activities such as football, rugby, and boxing, will at least temporarily weaken one's aggressiveness. However, a more social psychological conceptualization of man—one that does not necessarily subscribe to man's innately aggressive nature —might see existing sport programs as a force fostering violence and aggression rather than as one attenuating them. College and professional football—with the instant replay camera emphasizing red-dogging and blitzing, and the star player being given names of endearment such as Mad-Dog—is an institutionalized romanticization of violence. During my undergraduate years as an athlete at Syracuse University, I often heard Ben Schwartzwalder, the head coach, scream at football players who had already been practicing for two to three hours that the scrimmage would not end until he saw some blood. Much to my amazement, I discovered that Schwartzwalder meant exactly what he said. While the newspapers heap acclaim upon the most skillful athletes, the players and coaches often recognize the most violent and brutal players as the real heroes.

We reward and condone violence and aggression among youth, and then when as adults these people behave violently and aggressively, we blame it on man's animalistic nature! Even granting the assumption that man does possess aggressive instincts, it certainly makes sense from both a personal and social perspective to release one's aggressiveness on an inanimate object such as a punching bag rather than on the body of another human being. And if we are going to have body-contact sports, the emphasis should at least be on skill and proficiency rather than on blatant brutality as it so often is today.

Dr. Moore's psychoanalytic interpretation of sport as a harmless social outlet not only for the players' aggressions but also for the fans' is an excellent example of how a singular dogmatic theoretical conceptualization of the world can blind one to clearly demonstrable facts. Contrary to Moore's observations, outbreaks of violence and mass rioting at sporting events are all too common phenomena throughout the world. Race riots, from the national rioting after Jack Johnson, the first black heavyweight champion, beat Jim Jeffries in Reno, Nevada, on July 4, 1910, to the 1962 riot in Washington, D.C. following the city's high school football championship game, a riot in which 512 people were injured, have occurred with saddening regularity in America. Today, the situation has deteriorated to such an extent that nearly every major city in the United States prohibits evening athletic contests for high school teams. And sporting riots are in no way a uniquely American phenomena. The frequent mass rioting at soccer matches in South America and Europe often involve a level of violence seldom seen in America; Europeans call it soccermania. The violence surrounding England's soccer matches apparently is not limited to the stadium. A report prepared by seven British doctors reveals, "There is some evidence that hooliganism may invade the home after the match. . . . Some wives apparently live in dread of Saturdays and wait apprehensively to see what mood their husbands will return home in after the football match. If the local side loses, a wife may fear her husband will return home the worse for drink and give her a thrashing to get rid of the anger he feels about the lost game" (Goodhart and Chataway, 1968, p. 143).

One point that critics and defenders of intercollegiate athletics agree on is that participation in organized college sport is excellent preparation for the military. A Soviet writer, A. Kuleshov, quotes General Eisenhower as admitting, ". . . the true mission of American sports is to prepare young people for war" (quoted in Morton, 1963, p. 109). Perhaps recognizing the political ramifications of this statement, Eisenhower denied he had made it. But General Douglas MacArthur, a more forthright individual, openly and proudly speaks of the relationship between athletics and war (quoted in Moore, 1966, p. 63):

> Upon the fields of friendly strife
> Are sown the seeds
> That, upon other fields, on other days,
> Will bear the fruits of victory.

The United States Military Academy, the beloved alma mater of both Eisenhower and MacArthur, recognizes this relationship; consequently, it has the most comprehensive athletic program of any American institution of higher learning. Every cadet at West Point is required to actively participate in athletics.

The emphasis in American society on sport participation as preparation for military service prompted the great Russian writer Maxim Gorky to comment, "In bourgeois states they utilize sport to produce cannon fodder" (quoted in Goodhart and Chataway, 1968, p. 80). Although Gorky's statement may seem strident, many high school and college students who are rebelling against the authoritarian, militaristic nature of organized sport in America today would probably agree with him.

Along with the financial considerations discussed in this chapter, the development of intercollegiate athletics in the United States has been influenced most directly by two of the historical traditions mentioned in the preceding chapter. The Spartan tradition with its emphasis on sport as preparation for the military has had such an effect that according to Ogilvie and Tutko, college coaches make up one of the most authoritarian groups in American society, often out-ranking policemen and career military officers. Dr. Max Rafferty, in his speech reprinted in Chapter 2, openly and proudly discusses the inter-relationship between athletics and the military. And as I have already mentioned, the British tradition of sports as a means of inculcating youth with moral character has influenced intercollegiate athletics to such an extent that it now serves as one

(Wide World Photos)

of the major justifications for athletic programs within our educational institutions. Sadly, the concept that sports should be enjoyable and fun for the participants has had little or no effect on the growth and development of intercollegiate athletics in the United States.

"Upon the fields of friendly strife
Are sown the seeds
That, upon other fields, on other days
Will bear the fruits of victory."

15

Athletics and Social Mobility

There is one remaining argument often presented in defense of professionalized intercollegiate athletics, and I would be remiss if I did not discuss it. Liberal historians and athletic publicists, while sometimes admitting the abuses of college athletics, unanimously agree that intercollegiate athletics have been one of the best avenues for social advancement in American society. Apologist writers regularly point out with great pride how Walter Camp's All-American football selections had become democratized by 1904. Previous to that time Camp's selections were limited to Mayflower names such as Cabot, Cushing, Appleton, or Brooks, but in 1904 Pierkarski of Penn was selected to the team (Riesman and Denny, 1951, pp. 309–319, and Rudolph, 1962, p. 378).

College athletics have of course been a means of social advancement for many individuals from lower socio-economic groups, but this advancement has been little different from most other improvements in our society—a few individuals advance at the expense of large numbers of less fortunate citizens. Frederick Rudolph, in *The American College and University,* proudly says, "Eventually football would enable a whole generation of young men in the coal fields of Pennsylvania to turn their backs on the mines that had employed their fathers" (1962, p. 378). To put it politely, Rudolph is full of patriotic exaggeration. I make this statement as one who "escaped" an eastern Pennsylvania coal-mining town through the assistance of an athletic scholarship. My high school produced some of the finest athletic teams in the State, yet few of my teammates found athletics to be a means for social advancement. Yearly, close to two hundred athletes at my school would base their lives around varsity athletics, but at most only three or four individuals would be rewarded with athletic scholarships. The results of some statistical surveys reported in the Scorecard section of the September 29, 1969, issue of *Sports Illustrated* substantiate my personal observation. In the fall of 1968, there were well over 900,000 athletes participating in interscholastic football, yet less than 30,000 participating in intercollegiate football (p. 9). Since only about half of the 30,000 college players are receiving athletic scholarships, it is evident that less than 2% of all high school players eventually receive a college football scholarship. Schoolboys who spend four years of high school dreaming of collegiate gridiron glory are suddenly confronted by reality on graduation day. For every Broadway Joe Namath there are hundreds of sad, disillusioned men standing on the street corners and sitting in the beer halls of Pennsylvania towns such as Scranton, Beaver Falls, and Altoona.

The myth of sports being an excellent means of social advancement for black people has been fully exposed by such publications as *Newsweek* and *Sports Illustrated,* two magazines that are not noted for radical journalism. Sports, as presently organized in America, often exacerbate rather than attenuate racism. White folks have always liked to be entertained, so they will pay Lew Alcindor $1 million to play basketball, but to many white Americans Alcindor is still a nigger off the court. The hate letters and death threats that Tommie Smith and Lee Evans received daily during the 1968 Olympic boycott indicate what happens to black athletes when they behave in a proud, dignified manner.

The pretense of liberalism among white sport fans was exposed during the 1969 basketball season when the Notre Dame University basketball coach had the five black players on his team playing simultaneously in a game against Michigan State. The game was being played in the Notre Dame field house, and the overwhelmingly white student audience began hooting and booing any time the five black players were on the court together. The black players resigned from the team after the game, and did not rejoin the team until Jay Richard Rossi of Clarksdale, Mississippi, president of the Notre Dame student body, publicly apologized to

them. This incident is especially noteworthy since Notre Dame, headed by Theodore Hesburgh, a prominent American civil libertarian, is one of our most respected universities.

The disturbance at Notre Dame stemmed from the coach violating the quota system common in both American sport and society. Until recently, the quota system in a sport such as basketball usually allowed for no more than three out of the five starting players to be black. Or as Bill Russell has pointed out, ". . . it is longstanding policy to start two at home, three on the road, and five when you get behind" (1970, p. 82). This type of racist system takes its casualties not only from among black athletes but also from among principled white coaches. Dick Harp, one of the finest coaches in America, resigned as head basketball coach at Kansas at the conclusion of the 1964 season; he was upset and disgusted with the abuse he had received from fans and alumni for his starting four black players during most of the 1963–64 season (Olsen, 1968, p. 167).

The more perceptive observers of the American sporting scene have always speculated that black athletes were actively discriminated against even after the formal barriers of segregation were lifted. Aaron Rosenblatt, in a statistical study, the results of which were published in *Trans-Action,* confirmed the validity of this speculation. Between 1962 and 1965, black major league baseball players had a batting average 21.2 percentage points higher than the average white major leaguer. Rosenblatt's obvious conclusion was, "More places are available in the majors for the substar white player than for the comparably able Negro" (Olsen, 1968, p. 182).

It would be foolish, however, to deny that sports have not helped many black people to a more comfortable life. Despite how white people may feel about them, Alcindor and other great black athletes have their money and are free from the financial worries that plague most Americans, white and black. Gifted black athletes will usually make out all right, but what happens to the thousands of young unathletic black children whose only heroes are sports stars? How many brilliant doctors, lawyers, teachers, poets, and artists have been lost because intelligent but uncoordinated black youths had been led to believe by a racist society that their only chance for getting ahead was to develop a thirty foot jump shot or to run the hundred in 9.3?

Arthur Miller, a former athlete himself, poignantly describes in *Death of a Salesman* the pernicious influence athletics have had on many individuals in American society. Willy Loman, the protagonist of the play, reminisces at the end of Act I about his son who was a high school athletic star who never quite made it (1958, p. 68):

Like a young god. Hercules—something like that. And the sun, the sun all around him. Remember how he waved to me? Right up from the field, with the representatives of three colleges standing by. And the buyers I brought, and the cheers when he came out— Loman, Loman, Loman! God Almighty, he'll be great yet. A star like that, magnificent, can never really fade away!

But Willy's son, as have thousands of other athletic heroes, did fade away. For every white youth lifted out of a coal-mining town and every black person taken from the ghetto by an athletic scholarship, there are hundreds of other lower-class youths who have wasted their lives futilely preparing to be a sports star.

Even those few lower-class youths who do become proficient athletes while in high school do not aways find sport to be an avenue for social advancement. While college athletics facilitated social advancement for many second- and third-generation Americans from the 1890's to roughly the late 1940's, today, existing regulations of the professional basketball and football leagues discriminate against the majority of lower-class youths, most of whom are not prepared to enter college. The National Football League, the National Basketball Association, and the American Basketball Association all have a rule—called the "four-year rule"—that prevents them from signing a college athlete unless he meets one of the following three criteria: (1) possesses a college degree; (2) has had his intercollegiate eligibility expire; (3) a period of four years has expired since he first enrolled in college. This rule even applies to high school athletes who do not go to college, either because they do not want to or because they cannot get admitted; they are not eligible to sign a professional contract until *four* years after they were graduated from high school. Ostensibly this rule is supposed to encourage college athletes to complete their education before signing to play professional athletics. But since the rule's prime concern is athletic eligibility, not college graduation, its main effect is to insure college coaches that they will not lose their star athletes prematurely to the professionals. Before this ruling was made, many college athletic stars were leaving school to sign lucrative professional contracts even though they still had intercollegiate athletic eligibility left.

A further analysis of the "four-year rule" reveals much about the NCAA, the governing body of intercollegiate athletics in America.[1] The NCAA was able to extract this seemingly one-sided agreement from the wealthy professional owners in exchange for allowing college football and basketball programs to serve as *de facto* farm systems for the professional leagues. Consequently, the owners of professional football and basketball franchises, unlike professional baseball owners, do not have to spend millions of dollars on a minor league system in order to groom future major leaguers. This service is provided free of charge by our professionalized intercollegiate athletic departments. And since athletes are not eligible to sign a professional contract until at least four years after they have been graduated from high school, college athletic departments can get away with paying them anywhere from $500 to $3000 per year in the form of an athletic scholarship even though they are often spending as much time on athletics as full-time professional athletes. Lew Alcindor told me during his senior year of college that, excluding the better competition, the major difference between playing for UCLA and the Milwaukee Bucks would be that he would be paid well over $150,000 per year instead of $100

1. James Ridgeway, in his revealing book, *The Closed Corporation: American Universities in Crisis,* discusses an interesting involvement of the NCAA, the alleged moral guardian of college athletics. "In their desire for revenue, the NCAA in 1967, despite the opposition of the Ivy League colleges, voted overwhelmingly to accept cigarette advertising during the televising of college football games. The contract says that advertisers 'shall not include drugs which are habit-forming, patent medicines, tonics of dubious purpose, laxatives, political organizations or organizations whose policies or purposes are controversial.' Dartmouth believed that if laxatives were banned, surely tobacco ads also ought to be banned, since smoking was a danger to health. R. J. Reynolds, however, takes three minutes per game at $47,000 a minute" (1968, p. 94).

a month plus tuition, the maximum amount the NCAA allows an athlete to receive. And Paul Brechler, the athletic director at the University of California at Berkeley, candidly and proudly says that the only major difference between the operation of Cal's football program and that of the San Francisco Forty-Niners is that all of his players are college students. When I asked him if another perhaps more critical difference was not the amount of payment the two groups of players received, he quickly forgot about professionalism and made some unintelligible utterances to the effect that "our boys are amateurs." From college athletic departments to Amateur Athletic Unions, many groups are making money from the labors of amateur athletes—athletes who themselves are permanently barred from amateur sport if they take a few dollars too much expense money.

The "four-year rule" saves professional football and basketball owners literally millions of dollars, and at the same time it allows college athletic departments to have professionalized intercollegiate athletic teams without having to pay their employees competitive wages. Athletes have the choice of playing as professionals for the meager wages of an athletic scholarship for four years, giving up sports, or, as a few great high school athletes such as Cookie Gilchrist have done, leaving for Canada or some other foreign country where they are eligible to play as professionals. Most of them of course choose to take the athletic scholarships; consequently, there are many muscular young men on our college campuses who have no real interest in being there except for athletics. It is this type of athlete that helps to perpetuate the myth that athletics and education are inimical pursuits—a myth so pervasive in American academia that it has been able to influence the thinking of no less an educator than Robert Hutchins (1936).

While the "four-year rule" has proved most profitable for the already wealthy professional football and basketball owners and college athletic departments, it has in no way been of assistance to young athletes. It has in effect made four years attendance at college a prerequisite for employment as a professional athlete, the consequence of which is that sports have actually worked to preserve the status quo rather than being a means of social advancement for large numbers of lower-class youths. For, as William Birenbaum shows in his excellent book, *Overlive: Power, Poverty and the University,* and as numerous other educators have pointed out, our colleges are simply not designed to serve the needs of black and/or impoverished citizens. Additionally, even those lower-class athletes who can get admitted to our colleges are not always able to take advantage of athletic scholarships. They often have to help support their families after high school graduation, if not before, and they have no choice but to give up sports after high school and take a low paying job with no real chance for advancement. (A poor athlete has trouble supporting himself on an athletic scholarship, never mind a couple of brothers and sisters.)

The hypocrisy of the NCAA's claim that the "four-year rule" between themselves and the pros was instituted with the athletes' welfare being of prime consideration becomes explicitly clear when we look at the case of Spencer Haywood, a black college basketball star who recently signed a lucrative contract with the Denver Rockets of the American Basketball Association while he still had NCAA eligibility. Haywood enrolled at Detroit University shortly after leading the U.S. Olympic team to victory in the 1968 Olympics. Because of his reputation as an Olympic star and his outstanding ability, Detroit University officials were counting the money Haywood was going to earn for them even before he played his first game. However, after a year at Detroit, Haywood signed a $250,000 contract with the Denver Rockets when the ABA declared he was a special hardship case since he came from a poor ghetto family and had a number of brothers and sisters who depended on him for financial support.[2] Detroit University officials, completely ignoring Haywood's financial situation, were furious with him, the ABA, and the Denver Rockets. One Detroit University administrator called his signing for $250,000 "an atrocity" (San Francisco *Chronicle,* August 26, 1969, p. 44). Quite obviously, the main concern of Detroit University officials was the financial loss Haywood's absence would mean for their

2. In reality, the ABA chose to break the "four-year rule" not because Haywood was a special hardship case as they claimed, for scores of other black college stars are in similar financial circumstances, but because they were competing against the more established National Basketball Association and desperately needed a few big name box-office attractions.

athletic program. Haywood saw the situation from a different perspective: "Heck, I had trouble getting seconds in the school cafeteria. Imagine what would have happened if I broke a leg and couldn't play any more. That scholarship would have been gone real quick and I would never have a chance for the pros. I kept asking myself, 'What am I getting out of all this? The school is making a lot of money, so why shouldn't I be making some?' " (Berkeley *Gazette,* February 11, 1970, p. 13).

If professionalized intercollegiate athletics were abolished, there would have to be semi-professional farm leagues for the development of future professional athletic stars. In these leagues, athletes would be able to earn anywhere from $6000 to $15,000 a year while preparing for advancement to the major leagues. Under this system, the only requirement for advancement as a professional athlete would be one's athletic ability. The "four-year rule" and the NCAA's endorsement of it reveals the perniciousness of the existing system: those very individuals who are supposed to be helped the most by college athletics are the ones most hurt.[3]

The abolition of professionalized intercollegiate athletics and the subsequent rise of semi-professional leagues would be of benefit to all young athletes. High school athletic stars who do not have the ability, or inclination, to attend college would be

3. The "four-year rule" is only one example of rules that discriminate against poor athletes. Another rule which does this is the NCAA regulation that states that an athlete must complete his four years of athletic eligibility within five years from the date he first enrolls in college. If an athlete leaves college to enter the military, he is granted exemption from this rule, but poor athletes who are forced to interrupt their schooling because of economic circumstances are given no such consideration.

The following case in a typical example of how this rule works a hardship on poor athletes. In the fall of 1960, one of the top black high school sprinters in the country enrolled in college on an athletic scholarship. During the spring of his freshman year, he was forced to withdraw from school because he had to support a number of younger brothers and sisters when his mother became ill and was unable to work. By the fall of 1965 he had put all his brothers and sisters through high school and since he had continued competing in track, he felt he had an excellent chance of getting an athletic scholarship which would allow him to return to college. A number of schools began recruiting him, but when they learned he had first enrolled in college in the fall of 1960, they informed him he could not receive an athletic scholarship since he was not eligible to participate in NCAA sanctioned athletic competition.

able to become professional athletes and receive a decent wage for their labors. Athletes who were interested in professionalized athletics and who also wanted to attend college would be able to do so, but instead of participating in college athletics, they would play in the semi-professional leagues and be paid for their efforts. And with college athletics no longer used as a training ground for professional athletes, intercollegiate athletics would be reserved for legitimate college students who also happen to enjoy participating in athletics.

16

Alumni Influence

College athletics became a big business operation during the 1890's as pointed out in Chapter 14. Students did not have the time to manage million-dollar athletic programs, and faculties, still believing that athletics had little or nothing to do with education, were not about to spend their time running them. This power vacuum was quickly and eagerly filled by alumni, and today most intercollegiate athletic programs are still dominated by this group. Wealthy alumni availed themselves of the opportunity to control intercollegiate athletic programs for many reasons, not the least of which were the opportunities to identify with their alma mater's winning team and also to gain a feeling of importance and significance by being involved in such a well publicized university activity.

In exchange for financial contributions, the alumni were usually given control of the athletic programs. At Dartmouth College in the 1890's, an alumni group frankly stated that they would raise the funds for the construction of athletic fields if they were given control of the athletic program. The administration of course did not want to deny Dartmouth athletes the use of the latest model athletic fields: the funds were raised, and the alumni took control of the athletic program (Rudolph, 1962, p. 383). And the Dartmouth experience, though usually in a less obvious manner, was repeated time and time again at colleges and universities all across the country.

The conservatism that engulfs the American sporting scene

187

to this day stems in no small measure from the alumni groups that control intercollegiate athletic programs throughout the country. Not surprisingly, alumni who have the time, finances, and inclination to involve themselves in, and contribute to the financing of, a professionalized athletic program for college students are usually conservative men. Despite the existence at nearly all colleges of athletic advisory boards comprised of faculty, administrators, and students, it is these wealthy alumni who play the most influential role in the hiring and firing of college coaches and athletic directors. Berny Wagner, the head track and field coach at Oregon State, openly admits that coaches are not hired primarily to serve college athletes, but to please "alumni and other interested private parties" (1968, p. 8) who finance the athletic programs.

Just how do Mr. Wagner and other coaches please "alumni and other interested private parties"? The most obvious way is by producing winning teams that the alumni can proudly and vicariously identify with. Another less obvious but perhaps more important way is by molding young boys into clean-cut, obedient, yet competitive, acquisitive adults who will take their "proper" place in American society. The state controlled athletic programs of the Soviet Union turn out obedient communists, and our alumni controlled athletic programs are attempting to produce equally obedient capitalists. Walter Byers, executive head of the NCAA, understands very well that it is middle-aged men like himself who are the controlling force behind intercollegiate athletics. If Byers was really accountable to college athletes and faculties, I doubt that he would so regularly exhibit a "hard hat" mentality in his monthly editorials in the *NCAA News,* the official publication of the NCAA. Byers in his editorials makes explicit the conservative, authoritarian nature of big-time college athletics. In fact, Byers' editorials became so flagrantly political during late 1969 that *Newsweek* Magazine was moved to do an article on him entitled "Out of Right Field" (January 5, 1970, p. 35). But Byers himself continues to insist that college athletics are not political, and he regularly condemns anyone who attempts to inject "politics" into the intercollegiate athletic arena.

It is clear, however, that Byers thinks of "politics" as meaning those politics he happens to disagree with.

PRESIDENT NIXON visiting the Arkansas Razorbacks' dressing room after their 15 to 14 defeat by Texas during the 1969 college football season. Nixon appeared on ABC television while visiting both the Texas and Arkansas dressing rooms at the conclusion of the game. The President understands the present political nature of big-time college football, and this is why he never passes up the opportunity to publicly associate himself with the sport (*Wide World Photos*).

The following is an example of the kind of "non-political" editorials Byers has been writing for the *NCAA News* (April, 1970, p. 2):

Regardless of one's political persuasion, a true sports fan has to admire the punching style of the 39th Vice President of these United States. For speed, style and footwork, he does not compare with Sugar Ray Robinson, who had it all. Instead ring experts Nate Fleischer and Jack Cuddy probably would rate him with Tony Zale, the rock-jawed, indomitable middle-weight, who planted his feet, hit his opponent as hard as he could and took his very best in return. That is about the way Spiro Theodore Agnew of Towson, Maryland, took on the communications industry recently.

Judging from the fallout, the Veep's rapier right obviously landed where it hurt. The flak is still falling. . . .

The uproar caused by that hard punch from the Towson, Maryland, challenger (6′2″; 190 lbs.) suggests that some of our good friends in the communications industry protest too much.

An editorial in the December 1969 issue of *NCAA News* attempted to smear Harry Edwards, the leader of the black athlete revolt, and also implied that there was no legitimacy to the protests of black athletes that had erupted on over one-hundred college campuses (pp. 2–3).

The evidence is clear that there is operating in this country a hard-core revolutionary force designed to destroy the present gov-

ernmental and educational system of the United States. It divides
into a number of different groups and representatives of this movement have direct communication with Communist-oriented, revolutionary groups in other nations. . . .

Intercollegiate athletics is a prime target and vehicle for them
because of the publicity value inherent in sports and the fact that the
Negro or black athlete involved in a mild disorder will be a subject
of newsprint from coast to coast whereas the acts of a less-publicized
BSU party member may only be reported in the campus newspaper.

Alex Natan in his book, *Sport and Society,* offers an analysis
that succinctly summarizes the position of men like Walter
Byers. "It is significant," according to Natan, "that throughout
the world the only people to deny the political nature of competitive sport are those whose livelihood depends on such
lies . . ." (1969, p. 204).[1]

Dee Andros, the well known Oregon State football coach,
made a comment in the spring of 1969 which aptly characterizes
what seems to be the attitude of the NCAA athletic establishment. Andros, in a speech defending his dismissal of a black
football player from the team for wearing a goatee, proudly
proclaimed, "My policies haven't changed in twenty years"
(Eugene *Register-Guard,* February 25, 1969, p. 3b). Sadly,
Andros and his fellow coaches around the country have the
power, and will have it for some time. Our only consolation for
the time being is to remember that dinosaurs are now extinct
because they, too, did not adapt to changing conditions.

There would be little cause for alarm if the present NCAA
athletic establishment was just going to fade away over the next
decade or two. The frightening thing is that Byers and company
seem determined to destroy intercollegiate athletics before they
will allow sport to be wrested from their conservative, militaristic,
authoritarian grip. This is why the NCAA constantly attempts to

1. The AAU, the NCAA's counterpart for athletes who are not in
high school or college, is no less concerned than the NCAA with helping
to socialize athletes into mainstream, middle America. In an editorial in
the AAU's official publication, *Amateur Athlete,* David A. Matlin who
was at the time president of the AAU, discussed the philosophy behind
his organization: "We want, above all, to create a love for competition.
Today it is competition in athletics—tomorrow, it will be competition in
the business world" (Volume 39, Number 7, p. 7).

make itself synonymous with intercollegiate athletics. NCAA officials invariably make the claim that an attack on them is an attack on college athletics. Intercollegiate athletics thrived long before the NCAA came into existence, and if some degree of sanity returns to the college athletic scene, intercollegiate athletics may once again exist without the NCAA.

II

A cursory look at the past reveals how the moral lessons coaches teach college athletes are calculated to please the NCAA athletic establishment and its most influential constituency—alumni and conservative college administrators. In the late nineteenth century, alumni and administrators wanted coaches to mold budding entrepreneurs, and the coaches did their best to cooperate. Winning at any cost was the rule of the time; team discipline, sportsmanship, and other such matters, if considered at all, were of secondary importance. Professional athletes were

WALTER BYERS, executive director of the NCAA. Since college athletes have no voice in electing NCAA officials, it is not surprising that Byers—a man who was never involved in college athletics either as a participant or coach—is able to serve as executive director of the NCAA (*Wide World Photos*).

DEE ANDROS, head football coach at Oregon State. After dismissing a black player from the team for wearing a goatee during the off season, Andros proudly proclaimed, "My policies haven't changed in twenty years" (*Courtesy Oregon State Athletic Department*).

regularly brought in by coaches to bolster a sagging college team (Savage, 1929, p. 374), and since the ethos of the time was rugged individualism, a person's athletic prowess was usually evaluated independently of his personal behavior or appearance.

Robert Boyle in his Book, *Sport—Mirror of American Life,* reveals the extremes to which some colleges went in order to produce winning teams. "Seven members of the 1893 football squad at the University of Michigan were not even students, and Yale lured James Hogan, a superb tackle, to New Haven at the turn of the century by giving him a suite in Vanderbilt Hall, free meals, a trip to Cuba, free tuition, a monopoly on the sale of scorecards, and the job as cigarette agent for the American Tobacco Company" (1963, p. 22). A prominent critic, Clarence Birdseye, came to the following conclusion after examining athletic programs of this period: "Men trained in such methods through all the years of school and college life may become future leaders, but they will be leaders in the art of evading taxes, manipulating courts, and outwitting the law of the land" (quoted in Savage, 1929, p. 382). Still these were the type of individuals coaches were expected to produce, and produce them they did.

Today, our society needs acquiescent yet competitive, acquisitive people to work as bureaucrats in our bureaucratic-technological society, and coaches are busy changing the mold so as to produce this new type of individual. A few college coaches are old-fashioned enough to still insist on victory at all costs, but these men are a vanishing breed. The new coach is a bureaucrat, and his chief concern is conformity, not victory. In accord with this policy, athletes, no matter what their level of performance, are dismissed from college teams if they do not meet their coach's personal appearance and behavior standards.

Victory is of course still immensely important to the average coach, but it is no longer victory at any cost. The use of drugs such as amphetamines and steroids and the practice of keeping athletes academically eligible by any means necessary do not seem to disturb the sensibilities of most college administrators and middle-aged alumni and are, therefore, still a part of the cost coaches are willing to pay for victory.[2] However, what is usually not tolerated are athletes whose personal appearance and be-

2. Anyone who may think I'm speaking figuratively or exaggerating when I say college athletes are kept eligible by any means necessary should read the excerpts from Dave Meggyesy's book, *Out of Their League,* in Chapter 5. Only 50% of those few, select college athletic stars who make it to the pros bring college degrees with them. Yet somehow their colleges were able to keep the vast majority of them academically eligible for four years of intercollegiate football (Padwe, 1970, p. 69).

Athletic officials at the University of Texas at El Paso see nothing unusual about the fact that the five starters on their 1966 NCAA basketball championship team never graduated (*Sport,* July 1970, p. 67). And the recent cases of James Street and Pete Maravich reveal how college administrators work hand in glove with athletic departments to keep athletes eligible even when they are not attending classes. Shortly after Street had led Texas to a National Championship, including a Cotton Bowl victory over Notre Dame, he was allowed to drop all his courses without penalty only six days before final exams were to begin. Street, who according to an Associated Press story claimed, "I can't read a lick," had found the pressure of big-time football and nightly speaking engagements incompatible with the normal student activity of attending classes and studying for exams (San Francisco *Chronicle,* January 20, 1970, p. 43). Maravich, the all-time great Louisiana State basketball player, was suspended from school for cutting classes shortly after the completion of his final basketball season. But as *Sports Illustrated* rhetorically asks, "Since the cuts occurred early in the semester, one must wonder why Pete was not suspended until after the basketball season" (April 20, 1970, p. 9).

havior do not conform to the expectations of the NCAA athletic establishment and its supporters. The University of Kansas gave up an almost sure NCAA Track and Field championship in 1970 when they dismissed Sam Goldberg, their star decathlon performer, from the team shortly before the NCAA championship meet (see Chapter 10). Bob Timmons, the Kansas track coach, commented at a university hearing on the case that he had no complaints with Goldberg as an athlete, but what he objected to was Goldberg the person. Goldberg, who since has been appointed Minister of Sport and Physical Education for the Youth International Party, simply did not conform to the standards of personal behavior that Timmons was expected to enforce.[3]

The 1970 NCAA Track and Field championship that Kansas gave up when they dismissed Goldberg from the team was won by the University of California at Berkeley. But the actions of Dave Maggard, the Berkeley track coach, reveal that even having a winning team does not make a coach immune from having to cater to the tastes of an earlier generation. A number of outstanding athletes on the championship Berkeley team, including the team captain (see picture on p. 195), had what their fellow students at Berkeley would term fashionably long hair. These individuals and scores of other long-haired athletes have, over the past few years, demonstrated that long hair does not inhibit sports performance. The victory of Maggard's team was temporarily heartening to those sport observers who naïvely believed

3. Approximately five months after they prevented Goldberg from competing in the 1970 NCAA Track and Field championship meet, the Kansas athletic department announced that Goldberg had never been eligible to compete in intercollegiate athletics at Kansas. Goldberg had first enrolled in college in 1961, and, according to an existing NCAA rule, his eligibility had expired in 1966. The NCAA rule on this issue states that an athlete must complete his four years of athletic eligibility within five years from the date he first enrolls in college. Athletes who leave school to enter the military for a few years are granted exemption from this rule, but poor athletes such as Goldberg who are forced to leave college for a few years in order to support themselves and/or their families are given no such exemption.

The Kansas athletic department acknowledges that it was not until several months after they prevented Goldberg from competing in the NCAA championships that they learned his eligibility to compete in NCAA sanctioned competition had expired in 1966.

Sam Goldberg, decathlon star at the University of Kansas and Minister of Sport and Physical Education for the Youth International Party: "Our major goal is to liberate the athlete from the status of performer and elevate him to the status of artist. No rational athlete should be happy with the way he is treated. Our policy is to end the abuses and cultural prostitution of sport by any means necessary" (*Photo courtesy Rich Clarkson*).

that the struggle over hair length in college athletics was an objective question of whether or not long hair interfered with sports performance. However, much to their surprise, even Dave Maggard—the coach who won an NCAA Championship with a group of long-haired athletes—still asks hirsute athletes on his team to cut their hair in order to take some of the pressure from him. This pressure comes from administrators and alumni who will not be really satisfied until they get a winning team that also conforms to their standards of personal appearance and behavior. And if forced to make a choice, they will usually opt for a losing team made up of clean-cut athletes wrapped in red, white, and blue over a winning team comprised of radical, long-haired white and militant black athletes.[4]

The standards of personal appearance and behavior by which athletes are required to abide will gradually change as the attitudes of administrators and alumni change. For example, as a certain degree of hirsuteness becomes accepted by the general public, restrictions on hair length, beards, and mustaches will be relaxed. But even as these restrictions are being somewhat relaxed, one should not lose sight of the fact that college athletes are still being required to conform to personal appearance and behavior standards dictated by coaches, alumni, and administrators rather than by their peer group or their own personal tastes.

The influence of alumni and administrators extends well beyond controlling athletes' behavior and appearance, as most anyone who has sat through a typical college football half-time

4. One major college football coach, Chuck Mills of Utah State, has already begun wrapping his troops in red, white, and blue. Shortly before the first game of the 1970 season, Mills affixed American flag decals to the helmets of his players without first asking them how they felt about the matter. *Sports Illustrated* attempted to explain what motivated Mills to take this action (November 2, 1970, p. 13):

Utah State's football team had turned in its gear after a rather dismal 1969 season and Coach Chuck Mills felt troubled, looking back at the 3-7 record. More than that, he was disturbed because football was becoming more and more embroiled in social problems and politics. Utah State's football program had been involved in the problems to the point where it might have cost the Aggies a loss or two. BUT EVEN HIS TEAM'S PLIGHT WAS OF LESS CONCERN TO MILLS THAN THE CRITICISM HIS FAVORITE SPORT WAS RECEIVING FROM THE MOUTHS OF ATHLETES AND OUTSIDERS ALIKE (emphasis mine).

show can attest. Even at schools such as the University of California at Berkeley, Michigan, and Wisconsin half-time shows seldom reflect the attitudes and concerns of college students. And when in the fall of 1970 the University of Buffalo band decided to put on a half-time show that reflected student concerns, there was a great outcry from the athletic establishment. The game, which was being played against Holy Cross, was an ABC-NCAA regional televised game. Among other things, ABC, for the first time in their history of televising college football games, refused to televise the half-time show, claiming it was political. The show featured simulated "formations of smoking factories and exploding bombs while the band played such songs as 'Give Peace a Chance' and 'We Shall Overcome'" (San Francisco *Chronicle,* October 30, 1970, p. 53).[5] A few weeks after the Buffalo-Holy Cross game, ABC and the NCAA proudly televised the half-time show of the Army-Navy game, a show which featured the specially trained Army Rangers who had just returned from making a raid on a North Vietnamese prisoner of war camp that held no prisoners. Both Walter Byers and ABC of course insisted that this show was not political.

III

Until the last few years, coaches had little trouble getting athletes to conform to the personal appearance and behavior standards they demanded. As most any team picture taken during the 1950's or early 1960's would attest, high school and college athletes were a relatively homogeneous group. (And with a few notable exceptions, this homogeneity extended to personal attitudes and behavior as well as appearance.) But in

5. If the Buffalo band started what could very well be a trend, ABC might, before long, have trouble finding half-time shows to suit their clean-cut tastes. Eighty-thousand fans at the 1970 Cal-Stanford Big Game saw an unrehearsed addition to the half time show when Sam Goldberg, Minister of Sport and Physical Education for the Youth International Party, high-stepped down the middle of the field carrying a National Liberation Front flag. Goldberg took this action after Cal and Stanford administrators refused to allow even a small portion of the half-time show to reflect student concerns.

the last few years, the student movement and the growth of a youth-oriented counter-culture have contributed to making athletes a more heterogeneous group. The most obvious effect of the counter-culture on athletes is reflected in changes in their personal appearance, e.g., long hair, beards, and a "hip" style of dress. The influence of the student movement is reflected in an increasing number of athletes having a concern for their own civil liberties, a desire for meaningful participation in the running of their teams, and a desire to get involved in social issues beyond athletics. The turmoil in high school and college athletics over the past few years does not, as Walter Byers and others would suggest, stem from a clandestine communist conspiracy but primarily from the effects these two social movements have had on athletes.

Increasingly on our campuses we find athletes who are determined to think for themselves. Coaches and athletic administrators are not used to, and I'm sure many of them are incapable of, dealing with this kind of athlete. As psychological testing conducted by sport psychologists Ogilvie and Tutko has revealed (see Chapter 11), coaches are one of the most authoritarian groups in our society. Because of their authoritarianism, most coaches view openness or democratic behavior—the very kind of behavior more and more athletes are demanding from coaches —as a sign of weakness and would feel that they had lost control of "their" team if they behaved in such a manner. Given their years of unquestioned authoritarian rule, coaches like Paul "Bear" Bryant and Ben Schwartzwalder are about as likely to begin behaving democratically as is General Franco.[6]

6. Some college athletic departments have become so zealous in their attempt to dictate athletes' personal appearance and behavior standards that they are now demanding athletes sign a "contract" before they will allow them to participate in intercollegiate athletics. The "contract" Colorado State University at Fort Collins requires athletes to sign is typical. The following are only a few of the myriad rules a student at Colorado State must pledge not to violate before he is allowed to participate in intercollegiate athletics:

The athlete must at all times be neatly attired, clean-shaven, well-groomed and have an acceptable haircut. (By acceptable, we mean that it must be acceptable to the Head Coach of the given sport. . . .) While on or off campus, athletes are expected to wear neat and acceptable

John Pont, the University of Indiana's head football coach and a man who has the reputation of being a liberal coach, openly refers to himself as a "benevolent dictator." Since most coaches are malevolent dictators, Pont's benevolence apparently is enough to convince many sports writers that he's a liberal coach. It's a sad and frightening commentary on the state of intercollegiate athletics when a coach like John Pont—a man who refused to allow certain black athletes even to try out for Indiana's football team simply because he did not approve of their attitude—is viewed as a liberal coach.

The present struggle between athletes and their coaches and athletic directors is in many ways a microcosm of the larger struggle going on within the entire university between students and their teachers and administrators. In this struggle, coaches usually find themselves having to choose between two alternatives. One alternative is to give their prime allegiance to athletes rather than to alumni and athletic directors while also attempting to come to grips with their own authoritarianism. (To use a term I introduced in Chapter 11, the coach can choose to become the agent of the athletes rather than the agent of the alumni.) The other alternative is to take a hard-line stance and view all athletes asking for change as troublemakers. A few big-time coaches such as Harry Parker, Harvard crew coach; Mal Andrews, Hayward State College track coach; Dan Milman, Stanford gymnastics coach; and Jim Klein, Westmont College track coach have chosen the first of these two alternatives. Not surprisingly, most of the problems these men have encountered have not come from the athletes they coach, but from what I have been loosely referring to as the athletic establishment. The vast majority of coaches have chosen the second of these two alternatives, and this is why every big-time college in the country, with the exception of a few southern schools, has experienced either a major or

---

clothing. . . . Athletes are to use dignified and proper language at all times. . . . Frequenting of commercial establishments of dubious reputation is barred. . . . The opening of charge accounts is definitely discouraged. . . . There are to be no symbols, demonstrations or other displays of protest on the practice or playing areas or while a team is brought together for a team function. . . . The athlete will keep his shoes well polished.

MAL ANDREWS, head track coach at Hayward State College. Andrews, an alternate member of the 1956 U.S. Olympic team, is, in the author's opinion, the finest college track coach in America today (*Photo courtesy Micki Scott*).

DAN MILMAN, head gymnastics coach at Stanford University. As a college gymnast, Milman won nearly every honor possible: he was an All-American, team captain, NCAA champion, and a world champion. Today, he is making an honest and committed effort to adjust to contemporary conditions in the athletic world, and he seems destined to achieve the same degree of success as a coach that he did as an athlete (*Photo courtesy Micki Scott*).

minor confrontation between athletes and coaches.[7] The number of these confrontations as well as their severity will continue to escalate as long as athletic departments maintain a hard-line position and refuse to accept the fact that change is inevitable.

Athletic departments that recruit athletes who have not been significantly influenced by either the counter-culture or the student movement will remain relatively free of confrontations. Since the athletes at these schools will generally have the same values as the NCAA athletic establishment and its supporters, coaches are able to serve as the agents of both groups. Confrontations erupt when coaches have to try to be the agents of athletes and the NCAA athletic establishment, even when these two groups have different value orientations. In this situation, the coaches' position is much like that of embattled college presidents who try to please conservative boards of trustees while also attempting to keep peace with their faculty and students. More and more top athletes have been influenced in one way or another by the counter-culture and student movement, and wherever these athletes attend school—as long as the coach must serve the interests of the NCAA athletic establishment and its supporters—there will be confrontations.

It should come as no surprise to learn that the NCAA has chosen to support those athletic departments and coaches who have taken a hard-line stance. In 1969, the NCAA passed an amendment to its constitution which allows athletic departments to ". . . terminate the financial aid of a student-athlete if he is adjudged to have been guilty of manifest disobedience through violation of institutional regulations or established athletic department policies and rules applicable to all student athletes" (*Sports*

7. Open conflicts between black athletes and white athletic departments have erupted on well over one-hundred college campuses alone. By August of 1969, confrontations involving white athletes as well as blacks had escalated to such an extent that *Sports Illustrated* was moved to do a three-part series entitled "The Desperate Coach" (Underwood, August 25, September 1, September 8, 1969). While this series contributed little to the understanding of why these confrontations occur, it did document the extent of them. Unfortunately, for coaches as well as athletes, desperate articles such as Underwood's series will only make the situation all the more desperate.

Illustrated, January 20, 1969, p. 7). According to the San Francisco *Chronicle,* "This proposal, which some delegates felt was directed at bearded and long-haired athletes, barely passed by a vote of 67 percent, just over the 66⅔ needed" (January 9, 1969, p. 42). This ruling, which was also designed to keep athletes out of student protests, was typical of most NCAA rules, almost all of which are intended to control and limit the freedom of athletes.

The NCAA will pass rules that enable athletic departments to control everything from an athlete's hair length to how large a scholarship he can receive, but yet refuses, even after the Cal Poly airplane crash in 1960 and the Wichita State tragedy of 1970, to pass a rule requiring all NCAA member institutions to fly to athletic contests on regularly scheduled airlines. It is becoming increasingly clear that the welfare of intercollegiate athletics and the well-being of individual athletes is of secondary importance to the NCAA, whose prime concern is the perpetuation of the authoritarian, conservative, militaristic values of its chief constituency—coaches, alumni, and conservative college administrators.

17

Sport, Politics, and Education

The conservative, militaristic nature of intercollegiate athletics as dictated by the NCAA and its supporters has made sport one of the most reactionary enterprises in our society. The brilliant scholar Jacques Barzun, an administrator at Columbia University and a man whom one would expect to be opposed to professionalized intercollegiate athletics is not, for he is cognizant of how sports can be used to sublimate what he might term the rebellious strivings of young people. Barzun, in *Teacher in America,* discusses the role of athletics in education. "I do not share in the common view that athletics as such is the curse of the American university. It is better than the dueling mania, the organized drunkenness, and the other *social and political substitutes current abroad*" (1954, p. 206).* If Barzun had experienced the violence of modern football, he would not be so quick to substitute it for dueling.[1] But eliminating dueling or preventing drunk-

---

* Emphasis mine.
1. A little over half way through the 1970 pro football season, professional football teams had already spent over $2,000,000 on medical treatment for injured players (San Francisco *Examiner,* November 27, 1970, p. 97). The following remarks by Charley Taylor of the Washington Redskins about his college football experiences at Arizona State reveal much about the attitude football coaches take toward injuries (*Sport,* December 1970, p. 70):

"In spring training my sophomore year I broke my neck—four vertebrae. 'Hey, Coach,' I said, 'my neck don't feel good.' 'There's nothing wrong with your neck, you jackass,' he said. So the numb went away a little, and I made a tackle and when I went to get up, my body got up, but

enness are not Barzun's real concerns. Barzun defends professionalized intercollegiate athletics because, until recently, no Saturday afternoon football hero ever told Columbia professors that
they were guilty of counter revolutionary subordination. Barzun
quite obviously prefers Frank Merriwell, panty raids, and beer
busts to James Kunen, campus demonstrations, and students becoming involved in the running of *his* university.

Professionalized intercollegiate athletics is an integral part of
the modern multiversity, to use Clark Kerr's apt term for our
large contemporary universities. The multiversity, like all large
bureaucracies, expends most of its efforts perpetuating itself and
the status quo, and we have already seen how college athletic
programs contribute to these goals. The manipulative, authoritarian structure of our giant educational bureaucracies becomes
crystal clear when we see that school officials will not even allow
high school and college students a meaningful say in their own
games-playing—athletics. Instead of carefully nurturing the natural exuberance, passion, commitment, and idealism of youth, our
educational institutions dilute and, in the finished products, often
eliminate these characteristics.

Interscholastic and intercollegiate athletics are a microcosm
of the whole of American education, and the problems that exist
in athletics reflect the malaise that afflicts all of education. It is
just that the abuses of professionalized college athletics are more
salient and thus easier to document. Sport serves our educational
bureaucracies, and serves them well—perhaps better than any
other single activity sponsored by the schools and colleges.

In these times of crises for most universities, beleaguered administrators unrestrainedly show their appreciation for intercollegiate athletics. In the eyes of many administrators as well as
alumni and the general public, intercollegiate athletic programs
are the one area of the university besides schools of business ad-

---

*my head just stayed there right on the ground. And the coach says, 'Hey,
get this jackass off the field.' So the trainer put some ice on my neck and
after practice they took me up to the infirmary for an X ray and the doctor said, 'Son, your neck is broken. You got here ten minutes later, you'd
be dead.' Dead! Man, that scared me. I mean those colleges let you lie
right out there on the field and die. That's something to think about."*

ministration where neatness, orderliness, and respect for authority continue unabated. When the student body at San Francisco State (1968) decided that teaching ghetto children and assisting an experimental college were more important than intercollegiate athletics and refused to fund the varsity program, the San Francisco State administrators with the assistance of Glen Dumke, the state-wide college president, promptly came up with $20,000 to assist the athletic program. This incident occurred at the same time that San Francisco State administrators were telling black students that they did not have the funds to meet their request for the hiring of black teachers (San Francisco *Examiner,* July 15, 1968, p. 1). And the Regents of the University of California managed to give UC Berkeley's athletic department a $300,000 loan for the construction of a $550,000 press box at the same time they were claiming a financial crisis for the entire University of California system of higher education (*The Daily Californian,* October 22, 1969, p. 1).

Given the values that most college athletic programs are helping to perpetuate, it is not surprising that professionalized intercollegiate athletics and all its concomitant, well documented abuses are not only tolerated but supported by regents, boards of trustees, administrators, and conservative faculties. The administration of the University of California at Berkeley suspends some of its finest, most idealistic students for such minor rules infractions as using a microphone at the wrong time while protesting against the Vietnam war, but yet does little about the racist, authoritarian behavior of some of Cal's athletic coaches. And the Regents of the University of California, under the prodding of Governor Reagan, condemn the hiring of the aged Herbert Marcuse, one of the world's most famous Marxist scholars, but say nothing about the corruption involved in the running of a professionalized athletic program with college students.

The hypocritical position of authorities with regard to college athletics was further exposed during the fall of 1970 when an Oklahoma Civil Liberties Union official attempted to have the Oklahoma-Missouri football game banned, using the very same criteria the police and courts had used to cancel two rock concerts a few months earlier. Among other points, the ACLU official pointed out how it was necessary to have 400 more toilets installed in the football stadium if the same standards were applied to the game as the rock concert. But the Oklahoma authorities quickly forgot about law and order being equally applied and the football game went on as usual (San Francisco *Chronicle,* October 3, 1970, p. 40).

The examples of such hypocrisy are almost endless. Conservative politicians and alumni show little or no concern when "academic standards" are ignored to admit outstanding athletes. For years all major colleges and universities—including the Ivy League schools—have had one set of standards for regular students and another for athletes. Star high school athletes, black and white, have always been able to find some college willing to admit them regardless of their academic qualifications. But when conscientious educators set up programs designed to admit significant numbers of minority students whom society assured would not be prepared to pass "normal" college admission tests, these very same politicians and alumni cry out with alarm about the lowering of standards.

Football coaches such as Frank Kush at Arizona State and Jim Ward, the former Maryland coach, openly acknowledge they hit players when they get angry. Violent behavior by coaches— men who like to call themselves educators—is not at all unusual, although at most schools the head coach is usually sophisticated enough to leave this kind of tactic to one of his assistants. Violence by coaches is called building character, but when student protestors use it, even liberal faculty members castigate them by labeling their tactics neo-nazi. My point is not either to condemn or condone violence on our campuses, but to once again point out the hypocritical position of authorities with regard to intercollegiate athletics. Almost all politicians—liberals, moderates and conservatives—have condemned the violence of student protestors, but the last politician to show any concern over the violence in college athletics was Teddy Roosevelt when, as President in 1905, he threatened to abolish college football because of what he felt was excessive brutality (Rudolph, 1962, p. 376).

Most simply, the main reason for this double standard and

differential treatment is that the efforts of protesting college students are directed toward changing society, while the efforts of those individuals who presently run our intercollegiate athletic programs are directed toward preserving society without any significant changes. Consequently, the authorities take a hard-line law-and-order stance with regard to student protestors while at the same time they adopt an "anything goes as long as you don't get caught" position with regard to coaches, athletic directors, and their supporters.[2]

As the following quotation reveals, a double standard is normal operating procedure in all matters pertaining to intercollegiate athletics—even in matters of the utmost severity (*New Republic,* December 7, 1968, p. 11).

A city relatively free of civil disorders finally erupted into a major riot on the weekend before last. Over 6,000 citizens of Columbus, Ohio, took to the streets in a demonstration that lasted more than nine hours before it was rained out. Traffic on the city's main street was stopped; motorists had their cars walked on, painted, overturned. Store windows were broken. Police officers were manhandled by young rioters; bystanders were hit by flying bottles and bricks. And the mayor, who habitually responds to peaceful protests by sending in his club-swinging D-platoon, joined the festivities. Columbus newspapers, whose editorials quivered with outrage after hippies marched in Chicago, reported property damage without concern and pronounced the whole affair delightful. The police joyfully escorted the demonstrators. Governor Rhodes, who calls out the

2. Here is one more of the countless examples of the double standard extant in college athletics. The following quoted remarks are taken from the "Scorecard" section of the January 27, 1969, issue of *Sports Illustrated:*

Last November the University of Arizona confidently expected an invitation to play in the Sun Bowl in El Paso. When it appeared that Sun Bowl officials wanted to put off the invitation until Arizona got past Arizona State in its final game, university officials became annoyed and issued an ultimatum to the Sun Bowl people saying take us now or leave us. The Sun Bowl capitulated, extended the invitation and four days later watched ruefully as Arizona got clobbered by Arizona State 30–7.

With this in mind, it is interesting to read the following statement, which President Richard Harvill of the University of Arizona delivered the other day on the subject of student protests: "Making of demands and issuing ultimatums and attempts at intimidation are improper as methods of voicing views regarding policies and procedures."

national guard at the slightest provocation, felt it had been a great day for Ohio.

In short, this was a good riot. Well-scrubbed young Americans were celebrating the football victory of Ohio State over Michigan.

Less than two years later, the very same Columbus, Ohio, police force shot seven Ohio State students during demonstrations protesting the expansion of the Vietnam war into Cambodia. Shortly after this shooting, national guardsmen at Kent State—also located in Ohio—shot and killed four students during student protests over the Cambodian invasion. And for years, black students from Orangeburg to Jackson State have been murdered by police for taking part in demonstrations much less violent and destructive than the Ohio State victory celebration.

This kind of hypocrisy has not gone unnoticed by college students, and it is one of the many reasons intercollegiate athletics are increasingly coming under attack on our college campuses. Unlike during all previous attacks on college athletics, many outstanding athletes and even a few coaches and athletic directors are now in the forefront of the struggle. Hopefully, the presence of these individuals will help people to realize that the attack should not be directed at intercollegiate athletics, but at the NCAA athletic establishment and its supporters. The ultimate goal of the athletic movement is to abolish the authoritarian, racist, militaristic nature of contemporary college athletics, not college athletics itself. The struggle is not over whether intercollegiate athletics has a role to play in higher education, but to determine what the nature of that role will be.

Epilogue

Adequate remedies are not likely to be fashioned by those who are not hostile to evils to be remedied.

FELIX FRANKFURTER (1947)

There is no reason whatsoever to believe that the NCAA athletic establishment will in any way help to bring about the changes that are so desperately needed in intercollegiate athletics. To use Justice Frankfurter's words, the NCAA and its supporters are not hostile to what an ever increasing number of college students would agree are the evils to be remedied. In fact, the NCAA has a long record of actively working against allowing any significant changes to occur. As I have pointed out throughout this book, practices and policies that many see as evils to be remedied, the NCAA often views as its greatest strength.

Compared to their fellow students, athletes have, until recently, been a submissive, docile group when it came to speaking out about their own problems or larger social issues. This docility and submissiveness is understandable, for the athlete lives in a world where one misplaced word or action often means the immediate end of his athletic career. From Little League baseball through professional football, the correct attitude is as important as actual athletic skill, and once an athlete is labelled a troublemaker or uncoachable, his athletic career is usually doomed. For many years athletes perceived themselves as being in a powerless position within the sports world, and like most powerless groups, they survived by deferring to authorities—coaches, athletic directors, and professional team owners.

Because of the racism extant in American society and in the sports world, Negro athletes have until recently been the most docile and submissive of all athletes. The Negro athlete had no choice but to behave in such a manner if he wanted to survive in the athletic world. Negro athletes who chose to confront racist coaches and/or racist practices were almost invariably denied the opportunity to participate in organized athletics. But all this suddenly began to change when the black athlete revolt started to break out in 1967. The hostility, resentment, and anger that had been simmering for years below the surface suddenly erupted, and the black athlete revolt was headline news on sports pages all across the country.

The sacrosanct athletic establishment was now being challenged from within its own ranks, and by a group of athletes who heretofore had been the most submissive group. Choosing to ignore their own racist practices and policies which had helped to foster the revolt, the NCAA athletic establishment and its supporters generally blamed the revolt on some kind of clandestine, communist conspiracy. The NCAA's official line was that there was no real legitimacy to the protests of the black athletes, and that groups outside athletics were using the black athletes for their own political purposes.

The student movement in the United States was given its initial impetus by the peaceful sit-ins of black students throughout the South in the late 1950's and early 1960's. Similarly, the athletic protest movement that is now springing up on high school and college campuses throughout the country was first initiated by the black athlete revolt that began in 1967. Although the black athlete revolt by no means met with total success, the black athletes showed that when they worked together in solidarity they were no longer a totally powerless group. Educators and journalists ever since the early 1900's had been writing books and articles documenting the need for meaningful reform in college athletics, but the efforts of these individuals were, for the most part, ignored by those groups and individuals who controlled interscholastic and intercollegiate athletic programs.

However, since the black athlete protests involved athletes themselves, it was impossible for these protests to be ignored.

Looking back over the past few years, it is easy to see that the first real escalation in the athletic movement was the black athletic revolt. A mandate for change had existed ever since 1929 when the famous and thoroughly documented report on athletics and higher education by the Carnegie Foundation was published, but it was black athletes who had the courage to confront the athletic establishment on a national level for the first time. As we enter the 1970's, what is needed if the athletic movement is to continue to grow and eventually help to bring about significant changes is for all athletes to begin working together in solidarity. Throughout history, one of the main tactics oppressors have used to maintain their power is to keep the oppressed fighting among themselves. Athletes must be aware of this tactic and not allow the sports establishment to manipulate them so that they futilely waste their energy and time fighting among themselves. One of the main reasons the sports establishment has done almost nothing to attenuate the hostility between black and white athletes is because they know their hegemony would be threatened if black and white athletes began working together.

I would like to be able to suggest that the needed changes could be brought about by athletes working together with coaches and athletic directors, but it would be naïve and irresponsible for me to offer this as a realistic strategy. This approach will be possible at a few rare schools, but the sad reality is that most coaches and athletic directors are part of the NCAA athletic establishment and are totally resistant to allowing any real changes to take place. Still, athletes should recognize that there are coaches and athletic directors who are totally committed to the athletic movement, and these individuals should be fully supported. Among other reasons, these coaches and athletic directors need the support of athletes, for once they commit themselves to working for change in athletics, they will inevitably be ostracized by the athletic establishment.

Along this line, it was encouraging to see the support the University of Illinois football team gave their coach when the

Illinois athletic board fired him halfway through the 1970 football season. Working in solidarity, the entire team informed the athletic department that they would not play the remaining four games on their schedule unless the coach was reinstated. The athletic department could not afford to lose the revenue from these games, and faced with a united group of athletes, they conceded and reinstated the coach. The coach was eventually let go at the conclusion of the season, but seeing that the athletes were now a group that had to be reckoned with, the Illinois athletic department appointed four football players to serve on the selection committee to pick the new coach.

Athletic contests cannot be played without athletes, and the most powerful weapon athletes have in attempting to bring about change in a peaceful, constructive manner is the withdrawal of their services. In the Illinois incident, the threatened withdrawal of services by athletes got a coach they cared for reinstated. Over the past few years at schools such as Maryland, Providence College, and Georgetown, the actual or threatened withdrawal of services by athletes over what they felt was inhumane treatment by coaches resulted in the dismissal of these coaches. It cannot be emphasized too much that the reason these protests were successful was because *all* the athletes worked together.

During the 1970–71 school year, a group of athletes at the University of Florida carried the principle of athletes' solidarity to its logical extension by attempting to set up a union of athletes called the University of Florida League of Athletes (FLA). Despite the fact that the FLA was supported by individuals such as Carlos Alvarez, Florida's sensitive and articulate All-American football player, the athletic department was totally opposed to the union and fired an assistant track coach who had encouraged formation of the group. The Florida athletic department, with the full support of the NCAA athletic establishment, is doing everything it can to crush the FLA, for they know quite well the impetus it would give the athletic movement if the FLA meets with even moderate success.

Given contemporary conditions in college athletics, one of the most effective ways to bring about a situation where athletics will exist primarily for the benefit of athletes is for athletes to organize themselves in a manner similar to the attempt made by the

University of Florida athletes. The NCAA athletic establishment and its supporters will always be able to isolate and punish individual athletes who speak out, but it will be much more difficult for them to take this repressive stance when confronted by a united group of athletes.

A program of athletics for athletes cannot be outlined in specific detail, for the one thing it would not be is a preconceived system established in advance by a single individual. Such a program would be run in a democratic manner and all those individuals involved in it would have a say—from freshman athletes to the athletic director. Unlike today's static, authoritarian, tradition-bound athletic programs, it would allow for radical change in order to serve properly each new group of young athletes. As Howard Savage pointed out in the Carnegie Commission Report on Athletics in Higher Education as far back as 1929, "From the point of view of education, the most regrettable aspect of the control of college athletics in the United States today is the meagreness of the responsibility that is entrusted to the undergraduate" (p. 102).

St. Thomas Aquinas was one of the first thinkers to stress the value of placing greater responsibility for education on those involved. Besides being a sound pedagogical principle, student involvement in the running of schools is a basic democratic concept. Students are simply asking for a say in the making of those decisions that will shape their lives, and though this may present a threat to bureaucracy, it certainly presents no threat to democracy. We simply cannot educate democratic citizens in totalitarian school systems.

High school and intercollegiate athletic programs are the ideal areas in which to experiment with genuine student involvement in education. What do we have to lose by giving young people a meaningful say over athletic policy? From an educational perspective, the most dire consequences would be a few rather unorganized athletic contests. Student-athletes should have a significant say in all policy decisions such as the scheduling of games, the hiring of coaches, and the allocation of resources. The athletes themselves would suffer the consequences of any irresponsibility, and what better way is there for youth to discover the importance of mature, responsible behavior.

Appendix A

Sport, Politics, and Education:
A Case Study

As I mention in chapters 11 and 12, I designed and taught a course at the University of California during the winter of 1969 examining the role of athletics in higher education. This was the first time such a course had ever been offered by a college or university despite the prominent role college athletics have played in higher education ever since the 1890's. Few institutions are willing to rigorously examine themselves, and our colleges and universities are no exception. College administrators, alumni, and boards of trustees are especially opposed to educators probing the nature of intercollegiate athletics. But despite strong objections from the men's physical education department—most P.E. departments are little more than extensions of their school's athletic department—and no real assistance from the Berkeley administration, the course went very well.

Shortly after the course ended, I began receiving various job offers since I was in the final stages of completing my Ph.D., and after a four-month recruitment process eventually accepted a position as an assistant professor in the department of physical education at the University of Washington (see exhibits A and B). One month after I had accepted the job, and in the meantime turned down a number of other offers, I was notified that the job offer extended to me had been cancelled (see exhibit C). The faculty vote to hire me was 17–0 in my favor, but despite this, the Washington administration gave in to outside pressure and cancelled my appointment. I immediately flew to Seattle to confer with Washington administrators and was informed by Hubert J. Ellison, Vice Provost of Educational Development, that the pressure put on President Odegaard not to hire me originated within the Washington athletic department. While in Seattle I spoke before the men's physical education faculty which also included a few coaches who taught part time but were not regular faculty members. These coaches showed no interest in my academic qualifications to teach, but inquired into my association with black educators and athletes who had been prominent in the black athlete revolt. They were also extremely upset over my willingness to investigate and write about controversial issues in intercollegiate athletics. (Black athletes at Washington for a number of years had been protesting what they felt were racist conditions and practices within the athletic department, and the coaches seemed extremely nervous about my association with Harry Edwards, the leader of the black athlete revolt.)

The chairman of the department that hired me offered her resignation in protest, but the Washington administration persisted in overruling the faculty. This case confirmed what I had been saying and writing for a number of years about the inordinate amount of power athletic departments wield over the faculty and the operation of the entire university. I of course was not particularly overjoyed to have my own academic career sacrificed in order to substantiate what I had been saying. (A Washington athletic department official later informed a sports writer who inquired about my case that the faculty had learned their lesson and would consult the athletic department on any future faculty appointments that might interfere with the athletic program.)

I eventually filed a $350,000 law suit against the Washington administrators involved in my case, and shortly thereafter was extended a lucrative offer to quietly settle the case out of court. I refused to accept the settlement and am attempting to bring the case to public trial.

UNIVERSITY OF WASHINGTON
SEATTLE, WASHINGTON 98105

School of Physical and Health Education
Department for Women

April 20, 1970

Dr. John V. Scott
582 58th Street
Oakland, California 94720

Dear Jack:

It was good to have the opportunity to meet with you in Seattle and to introduce you to members of our faculty, the Dean, and Professor Lumsdaine. Subsequent to a conference with Dean Cartwright and in keeping with our telephone conversation, we are pleased to offer you an appointment as an Assistant Professor in the Department of Physical and Health Education for the academic year 1970-71.

The first appointment of an assistant professor is for a basic period of three years. It will be a nine month appointment beginning 16 September 1970 through 15 June 1971 with a salary of $10,500 or $1,167 per month.

Enclosed are papers pertinent to the appointment for you to complete and return to us.

We are looking forward to the opportunity of working with you in curricular developments of mutual concern.

Sincerely,

Ruth Abernathy
Professor and Chairman

RA/hah

Encls: Biography Form
Employment Notice
Request for Moving Expenses Form

cc: Dean Philip Cartwright

EXHIBIT A

582 58th Street
Oakland, California
April 28th, 1970

Dr. Ruth Abernathy
Physical and Health Education
Department for Women
Hutchinson Hall
University of Washington
Seattle, Washington   98105

Dear Dr. Abernathy,

Almost immediately after talking with you earlier this afternoon,
I made the decision to accept your offer. I have been most favorably
impressed by you and nearly everything I have seen and heard about the
University of Washington. I especially admire and respect you for
your willingness to hire someone "controversial" like myself. It is
unfortunate that we do not have more educators who are willing to
squarely face up to the very real and urgent problems of the university and society.

Would you please send me a school catalogue and any literature
you have describing the Department of Physical Education. Thank
you.

Depending on how the books I am presently working on go, I plan
to arrive in Seattle sometime during August. I am looking forward
to working with you and meeting the other members of the department.
Please say hello to Spencer Reeves and Jack Torney for me. I very
much enjoyed the frank, honest talk I had with Spencer.

Sincerely,

Jack Scott

JS/mm

EXHIBIT B

College of Arts and Sciences
Office of the Dean   May 28, 1970

Mr. John Vincent Scott
582 58th Street
Oakland, California 94720

Dear Mr. Scott:

I regret to inform you that I cannot recommend approval of the request of the
Department of Physical Education for your appointment as an Assistant Professor
at this time. I apologize sincerely for changing my view of this appointment
since I had authorized Professor Abernathy and Reeves to extend an offer to
you, subject, of course, to approval of the President and Board of Regents.

Your proposed appointment has created such dissension among the staff that,
were it to be approved at this time, it would seriously jeopardize our efforts
for an orderly integration of the two departments and for the changing of the
focus of the departments toward more modern developments in the field, while
at the same time maintaining harmonious relationships with the athletic
program. I am sure you will understand that I would place higher priority
on the rational development of these programs than on the appointment of any
single faculty member, regardless of the contributions he as an individual
might make to the field.

On the basis of your record of achievement and my interview with you, I
still feel that you will be a strong addition to any staff in physical
education. Please be assured that Professors Abernathy and Reeves and I will
be glad to offer assistance to you in seeking a position for next year.

Sincerely yours,

Philip W. Cartwright
Dean

PWC:ls

EXHIBIT C

The following excerpts are from press coverage of the incident.

UW DECISION ON SCOTT RANKLES MANY

Seattle Post-Intelligencer, June 9, 1970 (Frank Herbert). The University of Washington appears to have a tiger by the tail in the decision not to hire a humanist assistant professor from Berkeley for the new combined Physical Education Department.

There were strong indications the decision against hiring Jack Scott, 28, was made by UW President Charles Odegaard, but Dean Philip W. Cartwright of Arts and Sciences has been claiming it as "my judgment."

As a result of the decision, however, Ruth Abernathy has asked to be relieved of her duties as chairman of Women's Physical Education and other resignations reportedly were in the offing.

Scott, in Seattle yesterday to discuss the matter with UW administrators, has consulted attorneys on the possibility of a suit against the university. . . .

The American Association of University Professors has indicated support for Scott. . . .

Scott has become somewhat of a controversial figure in athletics after writing a book, "Athletics for Athletes." He took the position that "the commercial nature" of athletics should be downgraded. . . .

Ernest A. (Tom) Barth, sociology professor and a member of the powerful College Council in Arts and Sciences, criticized the UW decision. He said:

"Civil liberties issues are involved here. I want to know more about the reasoning that cost us this appointment of an eminently hireable man."

UW EDUCATORS SUED ON HIRING

Seattle Post-Intelligencer, July 30, 1970 (Frank Herbert). A controversial physical education instructor, hired and then "unhired" by the University of Washington, is suing key UW administrators and regents for $331,500 "for civil liberties violation."

Jack Scott, a doctoral candidate and former instructor at the University of California, Berkeley, filed the suit in Seattle's United States District Court.

The suit names UW President Charles Odegaard, Dean Phillip Cartwright of Arts and Sciences, Prof. Ruth Abernathy, chairman of the Physical Education and Health Education department, plus all seven regents. . . .

His suit asks $31,500 for breach of contract, $200,000 for injury to reputation and $100,000 for mental anguish.

Top UW officials were not available for comment yesterday.

The New York Times, June 29, 1970 (Robert Lipsyte). The system Jack Scott confronted may be even more formidable than the others. He challenges the values and priorities of intercollegiate sports, which in effect challenges this country's educational system. His book, "Athletics for Athletes," has caused a violent reaction among college coaches.

Scott, who has been teaching and completing doctoral requirements at the University of California at Berkeley, was offered a position in the Physical Education and Health Department of the University of Washington last April. He accepted. A month later, the offer was withdrawn because Scott's appointment would create "severe dissension" on the athletic staff, according to a dean's written statement.

San Francisco Examiner, June 5, 1970 (Dave Burgin, Executive Sports Editor). Some narrow-minded souls in the athletic departments at the University of Washington and U.C. Berkeley may end up paying dearly, in terms of unflattering publicity, for what they've done to Jack Scott.

He's the dedicated and deep-thinking young man who taught the experimental course, "Intercollegiate Athletics and Higher Education," at Cal earlier this year.

Scott was asked by the dean of physical education at Washington if he would like to go up there and teach the course full time. Scott thought it over, accepted, signed the contract and made arrangements to move in August. Last week he got a letter saying the deal was off, with the kicker, "Hope you understand."

Reason: Pressure from the athletic department at Washington. Give the Cal athletic department an assist on the play. Upshot is that the Washington faculty is up in arms over the fact that, once again, the coaches have reached out with a hairy paw and swatted Academic Freedom across the face.

Yes, Scott is radical, all right. In his book, "Athletics for Athletes," he blasts the coaches' mentality that makes the word discipline read obedience. And Scott doesn't think college athletes should be given pep pills and cortisone shots so they can play for Dear Old Siwash.

As a former athlete, he doesn't like the way today's students deride "college jocks." He thinks, or says he does, that the administration of college sports today is antithetical to the emerging life style among youth. But he thinks sports can be a beautiful form of self-expression.

The following telegram was sent to University of Washington President Charles Odegaard by officers of the National Student Association.

Charles E. Odegaard, President
University of Washington
Seattle, Washington

The University of Washington's refusal to hire Jack Scott to the physical education faculty is an insult and a further lesson to the youth of this country that Higher Education will not attempt to deal with the problems facing this generation. Scott's contributions to the field of college athletics are widely recognized and his perspective is one that is shared by a growing number of athletes and educators. His deletion from your faculty will be seen as an overt attempt to stifle the creative use of athletics— for the benefit of athletes—and direct it to the needs of commercial exploitation.

Lawrence J. Magid, Director
Center for Educational Reform

Charles Palmer, President
United States National Student Assoc.

Appendix B

Running as
a Spiritual Experience

BY MIKE SPINO

In 1966, after an injury put an end to my competitive athletic career and while still a senior at Syracuse University, I began coaching a few track and field athletes. Among those I worked with were Syracuse University's three best distance runners, Mike Spino, Marty Miller, and Ron Bukow. The track coach at Syracuse was an even worse than typical authoritarian, racist coach, and shortly after Mike, Marty, and Ron began working with me, they left the regular team, gave up their scholarships, and began training full time with me. It was a new and rewarding experience for all of us involved, and in spite of all the obstacles the Syracuse University athletic department placed in our way, Mike, Marty, and Ron ran the best times they had ever run and also began to enjoy running for the first time since their high school days.

Typical of the obstacles the athletic department placed in our way was allowing us to use the indoor track during the winter months only between the hours of seven and eight A.M. Much to their surprise, we used the field house every morning from seven to eight during the four winter months. I can still vividly remember having to hike five miles to the field house through four and five foot snow drifts at six A.M. one winter morning

when our car wouldn't start because of the sub-zero tempera-
ture. It was a love for sport, but sport on our own terms, that
kept all of us going during this most difficult time.

Mike Spino, who is now a high school English teacher and
coach himself, recorded a 4:09.8 mile in the spring of the year
we worked together, a time which was a new Syracuse University
school record and the fastest time of his career. I have included
the following piece written by Mike about one of our training
sessions in order to show the potential beauty and meaning
athletic activity can have.

Weather is different every day; running has its shades of
sunshine and rain. At Syracuse I ran daily in the worst weather
imaginable. Because of the hard winter, my running mate and I
had an agreement that we would never talk while running. Snow
covered many of the roads, so out of convenience, with only
slight variation, we ran the same course almost every day. After
classes we would return to our rooms and prepare to run. To
watch us get ready, you would have thought us looney. First,
there was long underwear, shorts, and hood. Next socks for hands
and feet and navy caps. The run was always better because you
could think of a warm shower, and know that the nervous feeling
preceeding the daily task of running would be gone.

Eastern winters linger into spring, but one day the sun shone
in a different way. Snow still curbing the road, but the inside
pavement, where the black-brown dirt met cement, looked
almost bounceable. Earlier in the day the spirit of approaching
spring made us, my coach, my running mate, and I decide on a
formidable venture. At a place beginning in the mountains and
ending in a valley near the city, we had a six mile stretch which
was part of a longer, twenty mile course. We decided to run the
six miles as fast as possible. The plan was for Jack, our coach,
to trail us with his car, and sound his horn as we passed each
mile. Marty, my running mate, was to run the first three miles,
jump in the car for the next two, and finish the last mile with
me. We traveled to the starting point which was out of the sunshine into the late afternoon mist. Jack suggested a time schedule
he thought we could run. I was sure I couldn't keep the pace;

Marty said nothing, taking an "if you think you can do it I'll try, since I'm not running the whole way" attitude.

Almost even before we started, cars began to back up behind Jack's car, but he continued to drive directly behind us, and the cars soon tired of sounding horns and drove around all three of us. From my first step I felt lighter and looser than ever before. My thin shirt clung to me, and I felt like a skeleton flying down a wind tunnel. My times at the mile and two miles were so fast that I almost felt I was cheating, or had taken some unfair advantage. It was like getting a new body that no one else had heard about. My mind was so crystal clear I could have held a conversation. The only sensation was the rhythm and the beat; all perfectly natural, all and everything part of everything else. Marty told me later that he could feel the power I was radiating. He said I was frightening.

Marty jumped back into the car. There were three miles to go; it was still pure pleasure. A car darted from a side street, I had to decide how to react, and do it, both at the same time. I decided to outrun the car to the end of the intersection. The car skidded and almost hit Jack's car, but somehow we got out of danger and had two miles to run. The end of the fourth and the start of the fifth mile was the beginning of crisis. My legs lost their bounce: I struggled to keep my arms low, so they wouldn't swing across my chest and cut off the free passage of air. My mind concentrated on only one thing: to keep the rhythm. If I could just flick my legs at the same cadence for a few more minutes I would run a fast time.

Slowly I realized I was getting loose again. I knew then I could run the last mile strongly. Perhaps, there is such a thing as second wind. Whatever, Marty jumped from the car when a mile remained, but after a few hundred yards he couldn't keep pace, so he jumped back in.

In the last half mile something happened which may have occurred only one or two times before or since. Furiously I ran; time lost all semblance of meaning. Distance, time, motion were all one. There were myself, the cement, a vague feeling of legs, and the coming dusk. I tore on. Jack had planned to sound the horn first when a quarter mile remained, and then again at the completion of the six miles. The first sound barely reached my consciousness. My running was a pouring feeling. The final horn sounded. I kept on running. I could have run and run. Perhaps I had experienced a physiological change, but whatever, it was magic. I came to the side of the road and gazed, with a sort of bewilderment, at my friends. I sat on the side of the road and cried tears of joy and sorrow. Joy at being alive; sorrow for a vague feeling of temporalness, and a knowledge of the impossibility of giving this experience to anyone.

We got back into the car and drove. Everyone knew something special, strange, and mystically wonderful had happened. At first no one spoke. Jack reminded us that the time I had run was phenomenal compared to my previous times. At first we thought Jack's odometer might be incorrect, so we drove to a local track and measured a quarter mile. It measured correctly. On the way home, I asked Jack if he would stop at a grass field, near our house. I wanted to savor the night air; I wanted to see if the feeling remained. It did, and it didn't. I have never understood what occurred that late afternoon: whether it was just a fine run, combined with dusk, as winter was finally breaking, or finding out who and what I was through a perfect expression of my own art form. It still remains a mystery.

Supplemental Reading

The following books and articles are excellent supplemental reading material for anyone who would like to get a more complete understanding of the role sport plays in contemporary American Society.

Axthelm, Pete. "The Angry Black Athlete." *Newsweek* (July 15, 1968), 56–60.

————. *The City Game*. New York: Harper's Magazine Press, 1970.

Beisser, Arnold R. *The Madness in Sport*. New York: Appleton-Century-Crofts, 1967.

Benagh, Jim. "Case Study of a College Coach." *Sport* (July, 1970), 32–35, 74–77.

Berkow, Ira. Five-part series on the state of intercollegiate football. Available from the Newspaper Enterprise Assoc., 230 Park Ave., New York, N.Y., 1970.

Bouton, Jim. "A Mission in Mexico City." *Sport* (August, 1969), 64–65.

Edwards, Harry. *The Revolt of the Black Athlete*. New York: The Free Press, 1969.

Gilbert, Bil. Three-part series on drugs in sport. *Sports Illustrated* (June 23, June 30, July 7, 1969), 64–72; 30–42; 30–35.

Henderson, Joe. *Thoughts on the Run*. Mountain View, Calif.: The Runner's World, 1970.

Meggyesy, Dave. *Out of Their League*. Berkeley: Ramparts Press, 1970.

Olsen, Jack. *The Black Athlete: A Shameful Story*. New York: Time-Life Books, 1968.

Padwe, Sandy. "Big-time College Football is on the Skids." *Look* (September 22, 1970), 66–69.

Rapoport, Roger. "Pro Football's Dropouts." *Sport* (September 1970), 54–55, 92–96.

Russell, Bill. "Success Is a Journey." *Sports Illustrated* (July 8, 1970), 81–93.

Ryan, Pat. "The Making of a Quarterback 1970." *Sports Illustrated* (December 7, 1970), 81–96.

Sage, George H., ed. *Sport and American Society*. Menlo Park, Calif.: Addison-Wesley, 1970.

Scott, Jack, and Harry Edwards. "After the Olympics: Buying off Protest." *Ramparts* (November, 1969), 16–21.

Shecter, Leonard. *The Jocks*. New York: Bobbs-Merrill, 1969.

Wolfe, Dave. "The Growing Crisis in College Sports." A two-part series. *Sport* (June, July 1970), 24–25, 68, 90–92; 30–31, 67, 69–70, 73–74, 76–77.

Zeigler, Earle F. *Problems in the History and Philosophy of Physical Education and Sport*. Englewood Cliffs: Prentice-Hall, 1968.

Bibliography

Adorno, T. W., and others. *The Authoritarian Personality*. Vol. I. New York: John Wiley & Sons, 1964.

Axthelm, Pete. "The Angry Black Athlete." *Newsweek*. (July 15, 1968), 56–60.

———. *The City Game*. New York: Harper's Magazine Press, 1970.

Bannister, Roger. *The Four Minute Mile*. New York: Dodd, Mead & Co., 1963.

Barzun, Jacques. *Teacher in America*. New York: Doubleday Anchor Books, 1954.

Becker, Ernest. *Beyond Alienation*. New York: George Braziller, 1967.

———. *Angel in Armor*. New York: George Braziller, 1969.

———. *The Structure of Evil*. New York: George Braziller, 1968.

Beisser, Arnold R. *The Madness in Sport*. New York: Appleton-Century-Crofts, 1967.

Benagh, Jim. "Case Study of a College Coach." *Sport* (July 1970), 32–35, 74–77.

Berkow, Ira. Five-part series on the state of intercollegiate football. Available from the Newspaper Enterprise Assoc., 230 Park Ave., New York, N.Y., 1970.

Birenbaum, William M. *Overlive*. New York: Dell Publishing Co., 1969.

Blaik, Earl H., with Tim Cohane. *You Have to Pay the Price*. New York: Holt, Rinehart and Winston, 1960.

Bouton, Jim. "A Mission in Mexico City." *Sport* (August, 1969), 64–65.

Boyd, William, ed. & tr. *The Emile of Jean Jacques Rousseau*. New York: Teachers College Press, 1965.

Boyle, Robert H. *Sport—Mirror of American Life*. Boston: Little, Brown & Co., 1963.

Brasher, Christopher, ed. *The Road to Rome*. London: William Kimber, 1960.

Brubacher, John S., and Willis Rudy. *Higher Education in Transition*. New York: Harper & Row, 1968.

Brundage, Avery. *The Speeches of President Avery Brundage, 1952–1968*. Distributed to the Press at the XIX Olympiad, Mexico City, 1968.

Cerutty, Percy Wells. *Athletics: How to Become a Champion*. London: Stanley Paul, 1962.

———. *Middle-Distance Running*. London: Pelham Books, 1964.

———. *Running With Cerutty*. Los Alto, Calif.: Track and Field News, 1959.

Chataway, Chris. "The Future of the Olympics." *The Road to Rome*. Ed. Chris Brasher. London: William Kimber, 1960.

Clarke, Ron, and Norman Harris. *The Lonely Breed*. London: Pelham Books, 1967.

Cole, Derek. "Future Trends in Athletics." *Athletics Weekly* (January 13, 1962), 8–9.

Connolly, Olga. *The Rings of Destiny*. New York: David McKay, 1968.

Cratty, Bryant J. *Psychology and Physical Activity*. Englewood Cliffs: Prentice-Hall, 1968.

———. *Social Dimensions of Physical Activity*. Englewood Cliffs: Prentice-Hall, 1967.

Cromwell, Dean B., and Al Wesson. *Championship Technique in Track and Field*. New York: McGraw-Hill, 1941.

Cureton, Thomas K. *Effects of Physical Education and Athletics upon College Men*. 213 Huff Gymnasium, Urbana, Illinois, December, 1955.

Cuthbert, Betty, with Jim Webster. *Golden Girl*. London: Pelham Books, 1966.

Devlin, Bernadette. *The Price of My Soul*. New York: Knopf, 1969.

Doherty, J. Kenneth. *Modern Track and Field*. 2nd. ed. Englewood Cliffs: Prentice-Hall, 1965.

———. *Modern Training for Running*. Englewood Cliffs: Prentice-Hall, 1964.

Edwards, Harry. *The Revolt of the Black Athlete*. New York: The Free Press, 1969.

Elliott, Herb, with Alan Trengove. *The Golden Mile.* London: Cassell, 1961.

————. "The Road to Rome." *Modern Athletics.* Ed. H. A. Meyer. London: Oxford University Press, 1964.

Farr, Finis. *Black Champion.* London: Macmillan, 1964.

Frankfurter, Felix. Introductory quotation to Chapter 5, "False Commitment." *Law, Liberty and Psychiatry.* Thomas S. Szasz. New York: Macmillan, 1963.

Frankl, Viktor. *Man's Search for Meaning.* Boston: Beacon Press, 1968.

Fraser, Dawn, with Harry Gordon. *Below the Surface.* New York: William Morrow, 1965.

Friedenberg, Edgar Z. *Coming of Age in America.* New York: Random House Vintage Books, 1965.

————. *The Vanishing Adolescent.* New York: Dell Publishing Co., 1959.

Fromm, Erich. *Escape From Freedom.* New York: Avon Books, 1965.

————. *Marx's Concept of Man.* New York: Frederick Ungar, 1966.

Gilbert, Bil. Three-part series on drugs in sport. *Sports Illustrated* (June 23, June 30, July 7, 1969), 64–72; 30–42; 30–35.

Goodhart, Philip, M. P., and Christopher Chataway. *War Without Weapons.* London: W. H. Allen, 1968.

Goodman, Paul. *Compulsory Mis-Education and The Community of Scholars.* New York: Random House Vintage Books, 1964.

————. *Growing Up Absurd.* New York: Random House Vintage Books, 1960.

Gorz, Andre. *Strategy for Labor.* Boston: Beacon Press, 1968.

Green, P. W. "Shamateurism." *Athletics Weekly* (October 7, 1961), 3.

Gretton, George. *Out in Front.* London: Pelham Books, 1968.

Harris, H. A. *Greek Athletes and Greek Athletics.* London: Hutchinson & Co., 1964.

Harris, Norman. *Legend of Lovelock.* Wellington & Auckland: A. H. & A. W. Reed 1964.

Hayden, Tom. *Trial.* New York: Holt, Rinehart & Winston, 1970.

Henderson, Joe. *Thoughts on the Run.* Mountain View, Calif.: The Runner's World, 1970.

Holt, John. *How Children Learn.* New York: Pitman, 1969.

Holt, John. "Some Thoughts on Education." *Edcentric* (September/ October, 1970), 10.

Hutchins, Robert Maynard. *The Higher Learning in America.* New Haven: Yale University Press, 1936.

Hyman, Dorothy. *Sprint to Fame.* London: Stanley Paul, 1964.

Jackson, Myles. "College Football has Become a Losing Business." *Fortune* (December, 1962), 119–121.

Jencks, Christopher, and David Riesman. *The Academic Revolution.* New York: Doubleday, 1968.

Johnson, Jeff. "McCurdy, Harvard Blend." *Track and Field News* (II April, 1968), 16–17.

Keniston, Kenneth. *The Uncommitted.* New York: Dell Publishing Co., 1965.

———. *Young Radicals.* New York: Harcourt, Brace & World, 1968.

Kerr, Clark. *The Uses of the University.* New York: Harper & Row, 1966.

Kidd, Bruce. "Canada's 'national' sport." *Close the 49th Parallel.* Ed. Ian Lumsden, Toronto: University of Toronto Press, 1970.

Kohl, Herbert. *36 Children.* New York: New American Library, 1967.

Larner, Jeremy. *Drive, He Said.* New York: Dell Publishing Co., 1964.

Lee, Gordon C., Ed. *Crusade Against Ignorance.* New York: Teachers College Press, 1961.

Lindner, Robert. *Prescription for Rebellion.* New York: Grove Press, 1962.

Lombardi, Vince. *Run to Daylight.* New York: Grosset & Dunlap, 1968.

Lorenz, Konrad. *On Aggression.* Tr. from the German by Marjorie Kerr Wilson. New York: Bantam Books, 1966.

Lovesey, Peter. *The Kings of Distance.* London: Eyre & Spottiswoode, 1968.

Loy, John W., Jr., and Gerald S. Kenyon, Eds. *Sport, Culture, and Society.* London: Collier-Macmillan Ltd., 1969.

Mackenzie, Marlin M. *Toward a New Curriculum in Physical Education.* New York: McGraw-Hill, 1969.

Mandel, Richard D. *The Nazi Olympics.* New York: Macmillan, 1970.

Maslow, Abraham H. *Toward a Psychology of Being.* Princeton: D. Van Nostrand, 1962.

May, Rollo. *Man's Search for Himself*. New York: New American Library, 1967.

———. *Psychology and the Human Dilemma*. Princeton: D. Van Nostrand, 1967.

Maynard, A. Lee. "Nature as Teacher." *Saturday Review* (May 17, 1969), 76–77.

Meggyesy, Dave. *Out of Their League*. Berkeley: Ramparts, 1970.

Merton, Robert K. Foreword. *The Technological Society*, Jacques Ellul. New York: Random House Vintage Books, 1964.

Metcalfe, Adrian. Interview in *World Athletics* (November, 1961), 14–17.

Meyer, H. A., Ed. *Modern Athletics*. 2nd ed. London: Oxford University Press, 1964.

Miller, Arthur. *Death of a Salesman*. New York: Viking Press, 1958.

Mitchell, Brian. "Character and Running." *Run Run Run*. Ed. Fred Wilt. Los Altos, Calif.: Track and Field News, 1965.

———, Ed. *Today's Athlete*. London: Pelham Books, 1970.

Moore, Robert A., M.D. *Sports and Mental Health*. Springfield, Illinois: Charles C. Thomas, 1966.

Morton, Henry W. *Soviet Sport*. New York: Collier Books, 1963.

Moustakas, Clark. *Creativity and Conformity*. Princeton: D. Van Nostrand, 1967.

———. *Loneliness*. Englewood Cliffs: Prentice-Hall, 1961.

Neill, A. S. *Summerhill*. New York: Hart Publishing Co., 1964.

Nureyev, Rudolph. *Nureyev*. New York: E. P. Dutton, 1963.

Ogilvie, Bruce C., and Thomas A. Tutko. *Problem Athletes and How to Handle Them*. London: Pelham Books, 1966.

Olsen, Jack. *The Black Athlete: A Shameful Story*. New York: Time-Life Books, 1968.

Padwe, Sandy. "Big-Time College Football is on the Skids." *Look* (September 22, 1970), 66–69.

Rapoport, Roger. "Pro Football's Dropouts." *Sport* (September 1970), 54–55, 92–96.

Ridgeway, James. *The Closed Corporation*. New York: Ballantine Books, 1968.

Riesman, David. *The Lonely Crowd*. New Haven: Yale University Press, 1961.

Riesman, David, and Reuel Denney. "Football in America: a study in culture diffusion." *American Quarterly* 3 (1951), 309–319.

Rogers, Carl R. *On Becoming a Person.* Boston: Houghton Mifflin, 1961.

Roszak, Theodore. *The Making of a Counter Culture.* New York: Doubleday Anchor Books, 1969.

Rousseau, Jean Jacques. *The Emile of Jean Jacques Rousseau: Selections.* Ed. and Tr. by William Boyd. New York: Teachers College Press, 1965.

Rudolph, Frederick. *The American College and University.* New York: Random House Vintage Books, 1962.

Russell, Bill. *Go Up for Glory.* New York: Coward-McCann Berkley Medallion Book), 1966.

———. "Success is a Journey." *Sports Illustrated* (July 8, 1970), 81–93.

Ryan, Pat. "The Making of a Quarterback 1970." *Sports Illustrated* (December 7, 1970), 81–96.

Sage, George H., Ed. *Sport and American Society.* Menlo Park, Calif.: Addison-Wesley, 1970.

Sanford, Nevitt, Ed. *The American College.* New York: John Wiley & Sons, 1962.

Savage, Howard J. *American College Athletics.* New York: The Carnegie Foundation for the Advancement of Teaching, 1929.

Scott, Harry A. *Competitive Sports in Schools and Colleges.* New York: Harper & Bros., 1951.

Scott, Jack. "The White Olympics." *Ramparts* (May, 1968), 54–61.

———, and Harry Edwards. "After the Olympics: Buying off Protest." *Ramparts* (November, 1969), 16–21.

Shea, Edward J., and Elton E. Wieman. *Administrative Policies for Intercollegiate Athletics.* Springfield, Illinois: Charles C. Thomas, 1967.

Shecter, Leonard. *The Jocks.* New York: Bobbs-Merrill, 1969.

Sillitoe, Alan. *The Loneliness of the Long-Distance Runner.* New York: New American Library, 1959.

Slusher, Howard S. *Man, Sport and Existence.* Philadelphia: Lea & Febiger, 1967.

———, and Aileene S. Lockhart. *Anthology of Contemporary Readings: An Introduction to Physical Education.* 2nd. Ed. Dubuque, Iowa: Wm. C. Brown, 1970.

Szasz, Thomas. *Ethics of Psychoanalysis*. New York: Basic Books, 1965.

————. *Law, Liberty and Psychiatry*. New York: Macmillan, 1963.

————. *Psychiatric Justice*. New York: Macmillan, 1965.

Vanek, Miroslav, and Bryant J. Cratty. *Psychology and the Superior Athlete*. London: Macmillan, 1970.

Wagner, Berny. Letter in *Track and Field News*. (I April, 1968), 8.

Williams, Jesse F., and William L. Hughes. *Athletics in Education*. 2nd Ed. Philadelphia: W. B. Saunders, 1937.

Wolfe, Dave. "The Growing Crisis in College Sports." A two-part series. *Sport* (June, July, 1970), 24–25, 68, 90–92; 30–31, 67, 69–70, 73–74, 76–77.

Zeigler, Earle F. *Problems in the History and Philosophy of Physical Education and Sport*. Englewood Cliffs: Prentice-Hall, 1968.

Index

235